Applications of Events Data Analysis: *Cases, Issues, and Programs in International Interaction*

JOHN H. SIGLER

Carleton University, Ottawa

JOHN O. FIELD

Massachusetts Institute of Technology

MURRAY L. ADELMAN

University of Southern California

SAGE PUBLICATIONS / Beverly Hills / London

Printed in the United States of America

For information address:

SAGE PUBLICATIONS, INC.
275 South Beverly Drive
Beverly Hills, California 90212

SAGE PUBLICATIONS LTD
St George's House / 44 Hatton Garden
London E C 1

International Standard Book Number 0-8039-0179-8

Library of Congress Catalog Card No. 72-84042

First Printing

Series Editor's Preface

A relatively new research approach—which began to attract increasing numbers of interested scholars in the late 1960s—has been characterized by Charles McClelland as the "international event analysis movement." The series of three "Events Data Conferences," organized and chaired by Edward E. Azar at Michigan State University in the springs of 1969, 1970 and 1971, markedly facilitated this development. A substantial flow of mimeographed papers emerging from these and many other meetings and conferences has been growing steadily. Most of these papers, however, have circulated within privately maintained communications networks among the participating individuals, and have not thus far been generally available to broader professional audiences (especially graduate students).

In an effort to make some interesting samples from this burgeoning literature more available, I asked the authors of the chapters in this publication (all of which were originally presented as papers in one or another of the three Azar conferences at Michigan State University noted above) to allow me to publish them in this format. This particular publication deals primarily with cases, issues or problems to which this research approach has been applied. A parallel publication (series number 02-001 by Azar, Brody and McClelland) focuses primarily on the intellectual antecedents and origins of this "movement," and some of its conceptual, methodological and theoretical components.

With appreciation for the generous cooperation of the authors of these two companion publications, I should like to stress two caveats on their behalf. First, although there are many points of agreement among them, each one should be held accountable only for the particular chapter or chapters to which his or her name is attached. Second, these writings were generally produced at least two years before their appearance in this series, and thus they do not necessarily take later work fully into account.

I especially want to thank Charles F. Hermann of Ohio State University, who is a member of my Editorial Advisory Board, and Edward E. Azar for encouraging and assisting me in developing these two parallel publications.

–Vincent Davis

April 1972

CONTENTS

Series Editor's Preface 3

Chapter I. Reliability Problems in the Measurement of International Events in the Elite Press 9

JOHN H. SIGLER

The New York Times 10
Cross-National Elite Press Comparisons 16
Conclusions 25
Notes 27
References 28

Chapter II. The Sino-Indian Border Conflict: An Exploratory Analysis of Action and Perception **31**

JOHN OSGOOD FIELD

Action and Perception in Conflict Situations 32
The Sino-Indian Border Dispute 35
Perceptual Data: Content Analysis of Political Documents . . . 38
Action Data: Rank-Order Scaling of Conflict Behavior 40
The Relationship Between Perception and Action 43
Predicting Behavior 46
Conclusion 49
Notes 52
References 54
Appendices 57

Chapter III. Crisis Decision-Making and Cognitive Balance **61**

MURRAY L. ADELMAN

Theories of Cognitive Balance 61
Multidimensionality 68
Perceptual Distortion 71
Exceptions to the Balance Model 74
Crisis and Decision Makers 76
Hypotheses 80

Data 81
Methodology 81
Findings 82
Conclusions 86
Note 88
References 89
Appendices 92

LIST OF TABLES AND FIGURES

Table I-1	Internation Interaction Categories	12
Table I-2	Intercoder Agreement on Decision to Code	12
Table I-3	Intercoder Agreement on Decision to Code Principal Categories	15
Table I-4	Intercoder Reliability Tests	16
Table I-5	Regional Coverage of External Relations in Elite Press	18
Table I-6	Rank-Order Correlations in Regional Coverage in the Elite Press	19
Table I-7	Coverage of Principal Actors' External Relations in Elite Press	20
Table I-8	Rank-Order Correlations in Coverage of Principal Actors in the Elite Press	21
Table I-9	Index of Injury	22
Table I-10	Rank-Order Correlations in Index of Injury in Elite Press	23
Table I-11	Index of Injury in Principal Bilateral Relations in the Elite Press	24
Figure II-1	The Sino-Indian Conflict in Systemic Context	38
Table II-1	Action Data for India and China: Level of Violence	43
Figure II-2	Indian and Chinese Violence Behavior	44
Table II-2	Action (S) and Response (R)	45
Table II-3	Predicting Indian Behavior	47
Table II-4	Predicting Chinese Behavior	48
Appendix A	List of Coded Documents	57
Appendix B	Indian Perceptions	58
Appendix C	Chinese Perceptions	58
Appendix D	Correlations of Perception and Action	59
Figure III-1	Configurations of Balance and Imbalance	64
Figure III-2	The Social System of an A-B-X Bond	65
Appendix A	The Perception Scale	92
Appendix B	Code for Document Content Analysis	93
Appendix C	Scaling Results	93

Chapter I

RELIABILITY PROBLEMS IN THE MEASUREMENT OF INTERNATIONAL EVENTS IN THE ELITE PRESS

John H. Sigler

A major problem in developing reliable knowledge in the study of international relations has been the relative failure to develop the discipline cumulatively, particularly in extending by replication important theoretical work developed on a limited number of cases. The methodological material reported here forms a preliminary part of a longer substantive study of the Arab-Israeli crisis of 1967, a study which generally follows the research design developed by North et al. (1963) in the study of the 1914 crisis and extended to the Cuban missile conflict by Holsti et al. (1964). The paucity of replication may stem in part from the failure to report more fully the specific methodological problems encountered in generating the data and to encourage others to work through these problems to provide more effective communication in developing cumulative knowledge.

The standards of the Stanford group in reporting on methodological procedures have been admirable, with thorough discussion of the use of

---

AUTHOR'S NOTE: *The author received invaluable assistance in generating the data used in this study from former students at Macalester College and the University of Southern California, who shared his belief that teamwork and replication are vital to communications and learning in the social and behavioral sciences. Particular thanks go to Gary Hill, Amal Itani, Chaqib Otaqi, Leah Wortham and Abdulrahman Zamil.*

the semantic differential in coding elite perceptions in official documents (North et al., 1963) and some discussion of the coding and scaling of internation actions (Moses et al., 1967). Jervis (1967) has provided a valuable critique of some of the validity problems associated with the analysis of elite perceptions in the Stanford studies. The material discussed in this paper is concerned with the seemingly more mundane problem of generating a reliable data base for the measurement of international events or actions. This concern for a reliable record of system performance or international behavior is shared by researchers with different theoretical perspectives, e.g., North and the Stanford group who seek inter alia to relate perceptual data to events data, Rummel and the Dimensionality of Nations (DON) group who seek inter alia to relate national attribute data to events data, and McClelland and the World Event/Interaction Survey (WEIS) group who seek inter alia to relate events in one time period or periods to subsequent system states.

Three preliminary problems present themselves to the researcher in generating events data:

(1) what sources to use in order to generate data appropriate for the design;
(2) what categories to use in coding actors, actions, targets, and any relevant contextual variables;
(3) what scaling procedures to use in constructing indices of system performance.

The present paper will concentrate largely on the problems associated with the first of these problems and touch only lightly on the second two which are, however, of no less importance.

THE NEW YORK TIMES

Attention was first given in the execution of the research project to the data already available from the WEIS project at the University of Southern California. These events data have been generated from a careful coding of the *New York Times* (city edition) for the period from January 1, 1966, to date. The WEIS group uses a nominal scale coding scheme which seemed to present the fewest problems in achieving satisfactory intercoder reliability. Preliminary work showed that coders could work easily with the WEIS categories but had considerably greater difficulty in coding events on either the Moses (1967) ordinal scale or the Corson (1969) interval scale. Both scales call for the coding of events data which include contextual variables beyond the "who does what to whom" format of the

WEIS scheme. These contextual variables include domestic internation events which have indirect consequences on another international actor. The selection of these events and their indirect (often unintended) targets calls for considerable judgmental interpretation by the coder. The ordinal and interval scales address themselves, however, more directly to the weighting of events, a persistent problem in the utilization of events data in measuring international behavior. Provided one has a sufficiently large number of events to work with, one can argue with Pool (1959: 194) that frequency counts are as satisfactory a measure of intensity or importance as any available alternative.

To increase familiarity with the coding scheme before extending the data base available from the *New York Times,* we undertook a complete recoding of the three month period from May 1 to July 31, 1967, to test the reliability of our coding against that of the more experienced WEIS coders. Some two weeks were spent in training coders using the codebook then available from the WEIS project (Martin and Young, 1968).

Before undertaking an item-by-item analysis, we compared the overall results for the three-month period using the major categories. We collapsed the WEIS 63 action categories into the 22 category interaction codes shown in Table I-1. Following the example of Janda (1969) in discussing reliability problems in information retrieval, we first used a "macroscopic" measure of indexing reliability which measures agreement in use of codes over the entire time period without being sensitive to whether the same item is in fact being coded. For this macroscopic measure of reliability, Janda uses the product-moment correlation which is calculated by treating the coders as the variables, the frequency with which both coders use a given code as values of the variables, and coding categories used by both as the number of cases. Such a measure gives no assurance that the coders coded the same items in the same way, but we know that they found a similar number of references to that category throughout the document coded. The product-moment correlation for the action categories shown in Table I-1 for the WEIS coders and our coders is .94. The rank-order correlation (rho) between the two lists is .80. In both tests, we find substantial macroscopic agreement in the use of these interaction categories over the three-month period.

Our next question was whether or not coders were finding the same items in the press. A day-by-day check was made for the months of May and June for reporting of the same items, overlooking for the moment whether or not they were coded in the same way on the same items. The results are reported in Table I-2.

For the "microscopic" measure of intercoder reliability, we again

TABLE I-1
INTERNATION INTERACTION CATEGORIES
(New York Times, **May-July 1967***)*

	New York Times			
	(city)		(late)	
Categories	Items n	Rank	Items n	Rank
1. Yield	14	(21)	12	(22)
2. Comment	361	(1)	258	(1)
3. Consult	259	(2)	299	(3)
4. Approve	48	(13)	44	(13)
5. Promise	50	(12)	38	(16)
6. Grant	72	(8)	34	(17)
7. Reward	35	(18)	45	(12)
8. Agree	90	(7)	107	(4)
9. Request	68	(9)	79	(7)
10. Propose	128	(4)	105	(5)
11. Reject	66	(10)	59	(8)
12. Accuse	227	(3)	250	(2)
13. Protest	38	(16)	42	(14)
14. Deny	34	(19)	49	(10)
15. Demand	39	(14.5)	16	(20)
16. Warn	39	(14.5)	22	(18)
17. Threaten	11	(22)	39	(15)
18. Demonstrate	58	(11)	85	(6)
19. Reduce relationship	94	(6)	49	(10)
20. Expel	19	(20)	14	(21)
21. Seize	36	(17)	18	(19)
22. Force	114	(5)	49	(10)
Totals	1,900		1,713	

TABLE I-2
INTERCODER AGREEMENT ON DECISION TO CODE
(New York Times, **May-June 1967***)*

Month/Day		Both Agree to Code	WEIS Code Only	Replication Code Only	Total Disagree
May	1	8	10	3	13
	2	3	8	1	9
	3	4	6	3	9
	4	5	8	14	22
	5	4	8	4	12
	6	3	1	3	4
	7	2	4	6	10
	8	5	5	5	10
	9	4	3	8	11
	10	5	3	2	5
	11	8	3	6	9
	12	3	2	2	4
	13	7	1	13	14

TABLE I-2 (continued)

Month/Day	Both Agree to Code	WEIS Code Only	Replication Code Only	Total Disagree
14	10	5	3	8
15	8	12	8	20
16	10	16	4	20
17	9	11	9	20
18	10	2	16	18
19	6	2	4	6
20	4	12	4	16
21	4	12	15	27
22	6	7	15	22
23	14	19	5	24
24	10	21	7	28
25	9	17	6	23
26	10	21	5	26
27	8	28	9	37
28	6	12	3	15
29	17	26	9	35
30	10	21	5	26
31	14	17	19	36
Totals	226	323	216	539
June 1	8	16	14	30
2	11	9	7	16
3	6	8	11	19
4	9	11	11	22
5-6	56	55	38	93
7	23	31	9	40
8	0	0	33	33
9	25	45	26	71
10	10	33	5	38
11	5	30	12	42
12	12	14	13	27
13	7	12	10	22
14	19	14	13	27
15	9	7	7	14
16	11	18	31	49
17	6	16	8	24
18	4	10	16	26
19	6	5	7	12
20	7	4	4	8
21	5	20	3	23
22	14	13	11	24
23	3	28	5	33
24	3	30	2	32
25	8	16	0	16
26	10	27	7	34
27	5	13	4	17
28	5	21	5	26
29	7	11	6	17
30	21	8	21	30
Totals	315	526	339	865

follow Janda, using the familiar coefficient of reliability ($CR = 2M/N_1 + N_2$) where M is the match or agreement on the same item and its coding by both coders, N_1 is the total number of items coded by the first coder and N_2 is the total number coded by the second coder. Interpreting M in this case only as the common decision to code the same item from the press, we find a CR of .42 for the month of May and .43 for the month of June. Simply stated, the coders are disagreeing more often than agreeing in choosing the same items from the press. These coefficients set the maximum limits for full intercoder reliability tests which will be reduced by the amount of disagreement on assignment of categories to the same items coded. We were considerably discouraged at this phase of the research effort, particularly in view of the intercoder reliability coefficient of .83 earlier reported by McClelland and Hoggard (1969) for their coding.[1]

Analyzing the same items coded and interpreting N as only these items, we found an intercoder reliability coefficient of .83. In other words, the assignment of categories was not an insuperable obstacle in achieving acceptable reliability coefficients; the choice of items to code did pose a serious obstacle. Applying the usual formulation of CR, we found an overall intercoder reliability coefficient of only .37 in comparing our collection and that done by the WEIS group.

The principal problems then appeared to be those of "threshold" decisions to code questionable items and carelessness in overlooking certain items. To explore this point more thoroughly, we calculated intercoder reliability coefficients for each of the 22 interaction categories as well as the 21 principal actors reported in the WEIS collection and our collection for the period of May through July 1967. These coefficients are reported in Table I-3. News items concerning the great powers seemed easier to code than those dealing with lesser powers in the international system. Some important interaction categories such as threat and acts of force showed surprisingly low reliability. Research which reports only an overall intercoder reliability coefficient when many categories have been used may be misleading unless the reader is assured that individual categories used also meet the minimum acceptable level of reliability. Some categories may call for more judgment on the part of the coders, and substantial disagreement in the use of these codes could be concealed by the use of an overall reliability coefficient in which these categories are submerged with many other codes with minimal judgmental component. In carrying out these tests, certain items involving the use of armed force in isolated instances in Korea seemed so obvious to us for coding that we were surprised that they did not appear in the WEIS collection. We then

TABLE I-3
INTERCODER AGREEMENT ON DECISION TO CODE PRINCIPAL CATEGORIES *(New York Times,* **May-July 1967***)*

Actors		Interaction	
1. USA	*.87*	1. Yield	.60
2. CAN	.70	2. Comment	*.80*
3. CUB	.57	3. Consult	*.89*
4. UNK	.72	4. Approve	.50
5. FRN	*.76*	5. Promise	.64
6. GMW	.68	6. Grant	.65
7. VAT	.46	7. Reward	*.75*
8. USR	*.82*	8. Agree	.67
9. UNO	*.81*	9. Request	*.77*
10. NIG	.45	10. Propose	.76
11. COP	.53	11. Reject	*.90*
12. ALG	.52	12. Accuse	*.80*
13. SUD	.44	13. Protest	*.78*
14. IRQ	.70	14. Deny	.62
15. UAR	.74	15. Demand	.45
16. SYR	.64	16. Warn	.70
17. JOR	.70	17. Threaten	.47
18. ISR	*.78*	18. Demonstrate	*.75*
19. CHN	*.78*	19. Reduce relationship	.55
20. IND	*.76*	20. Expel	.57
21. VTN	.55	21. Seize	.50
		22. Force	.55

discovered what perhaps should have been obvious to us from the outset—our study was not a replication of the coding done by the WEIS group; we were working from the microfilm copy of the *New York Times* which is based on the late city edition which appears later than the city edition, the one airmailed to subscribers outside New York City and the one used by the WEIS group.[2]

Not having the city edition at hand, we were unable to conduct the planned comparison between our coding and that of the WEIS group but instead turned to a reliability check on our own coding of the late city edition. The issues for the month of June were recoded by four different coders working on one week each and the results compared with that done by a single coder in the first phase. The results, summarized in Table I-4, were again disappointing. We were able to improve somewhat on the overall intercoder reliability coefficient from the two-edition comparison, but the results still fell well below generally acceptable limits.[3] We suspected that the two "participation" categories—comment and consult—may have accounted for considerable difficulty in threshold decisions to code. They also, however, were highly reliable in coding once the decision

TABLE I-4
INTERCODER RELIABILITY TESTS *(New York Times,*
June 1967; late city edition*)*

Groups	Coders A-B	A-C	A-D	A-E	Mean
Same items	.93	.80	.88	.87	.87
All items	.51	.37	.54	.64	.51
Adjusted items	.63	.40	.56	.75	.59

to code was made. Removing all comment and consult items from the list gave us an adjusted list of categories, and the coefficients were improved somewhat. Considerable differences among coders do show up in the analysis above and, with extended training, better results may well be possible.[4] These are the only tests which were conducted on the microscopic level for the sameness of coding.

This distinction between "sameness" of coding as measured by a microscopic item-by-item analysis and "similarity" of coding as measured by a macroscopic examination of overall category use needs further examination. It may be argued that it is not as important for index construction to deal with the same universe of events as with similarity in samples. This implies, however, far greater attention to tests for similarity between related and independent samples than has heretofore been the case in data generation on international events.[5]

CROSS-NATIONAL ELITE PRESS COMPARISONS

Hoggard (1967), Burrowes (1969), Smith (1969) and Azar et al. (1969) have reported that reliance on a single source for events data appears inappropriate for most area research questions. *The Middle East Journal* chronology, which Azar found reports more items for his 1956-1957 Egyptian sample than did the *New York Times,* appeared rather sketchy for our intensive analysis of weekly periods in the Arab-Israeli crisis of 1967. We decided to add the *Times* (London), *Le Monde,* and two leading area newspapers, the semi-official *al-Ahram* (Cairo) and the English language *Jerusalem Post* as basic data sources. We then compared the various sources on the macroscopic basis suggested earlier to determine to what extent the various newspapers are reporting a similar universe of events and similar coverage of various actors, their actions and targets.

Galtung and Ruge (1965) have suggested that the gatekeepers in the elite press are themselves immersed in complex hierarchical social structures which influence their perception of events. Working from their more abstract formulation, one can suggest a number of hypotheses about the structure of foreign news in the press:

(H1) Gatekeepers pay more attention to international news that deals with their own state.

(H2) Gatekeepers pay more attention to news about higher-ranking than lower-ranking nations.

(H3) News about one's own state will be reported more favorably than news about others.

(H4) News about allies will be reported more favorably than news about neutrals or enemies.

(H5) News from low-ranking nations will tend to be more unfavorable in order to come into the sphere of attention of gatekeepers in other nations.

The newspaper sample here is too small for any reliable test of these hypotheses, but the data reported in Table I-5 suggest that the press does reflect a bias toward more intensive coverage of one's own region. The *New York Times* reports relatively more events about the North American region than the others in the sample, the *Times* (London) and *Le Monde* more about northwestern Europe, and the *Jerusalem Post* and *al-Ahram* far exceed the others in detailed reporting on the Middle East. The fact that the Western newspapers also give large amounts of attention to the Middle East is associated with the intensive reporting of the mounting diplomatic and military crisis in the area, thus lending some support to hypothesis 4 that news from lower-ranking actors will tend to be more unfavorable. No test is possible without a comparison of these sources over a large number of months. Using the rank-order correlation (rho) as a measure of macroscopic indexing similarity, we find substantial similarity in regional coverage as reported in Table I-6.[6] Both European newspapers give slightly more coverage to Eastern Europe than to North America. Third world countries outside the Middle East receive little attention in all the newspapers.

Turning to coverage of the principal actors[7] reported during the month of May (Table I-7), one finds general support for the notion of primary attention being given to the news about one's own nation. The hypothesis holds for the *New York Times,* the *Times, al-Ahram* and the *Jerusalem Post. Le Monde* not only does not report France most frequently but least frequently among the eight actors covered. Whether this striking cosmopolitanism is typical is doubtful as McClelland (1969) has reported earlier that the WEIS sample of *Le Monde* for a different time period reported six percent more events about France than the next ranking actor in the system.

TABLE I-5

REGIONAL COVERAGE OF EXTERNAL RELATIONS IN ELITE PRESS (May 1967)

Regions	*New York Times* (early)		*New York Times* (late)		*Times* (London)		*Le Monde*		*Jerusalem Post*		*al-Ahram*	
	Item n	Rank	Item n	Rank	Item n	Rank	Item n	Rank	Item n	Rank	Item n	Rank
North America	179	(2)	178	(2)	82	(4)	86	(4)	129	(3)	199	(2)
South America	11	(9.5)	9	(10)	5	(9)	4	(9)	8	(9.5)	11	(10)
Northwest Europe	124	(3)	115	(3)	157	(2)	141	(1)	139	(2)	179	(3)
Southeast and Eastern Europe	103	(4)	77	(5)	92	(3)	114	(3)	108	(4)	162	(4)
West Africa	11	(9.5)	30	(8)	3	(11)	5	(8)	8	(9.5)	16	(16)
East Africa	14	(8)	23	(9)	18	(7)	3	(10)	17	(7)	42	(7)
Middle East and North Africa	267	(1)	266	(1)	189	(1)	133	(2)	654	(1)	1,068	(1)
East Asia	95	(5)	81	(4)	44	(6)	50	(5)	35	(6)	57	(6)
Southeast Asia	51	(6.5)	32	(7)	8	(8)	19	(7)	9	(8)	26	(8)
Oceania	3	(11)	1	(11)	4	(10)	1	(11)	1	(11)	11	(8)
UN	51	(6.5)	57	(6)	51	(5)	46	(6)	78	(5)	63	(5)
Totals	909		869		653		602		1,186		1,823	

TABLE I-6
RANK-ORDER CORRELATIONS IN REGIONAL COVERAGE IN THE ELITE PRESS (May 1967)

Regions	*New York Times* (early)	*New York Times* (late)	*Times* (London)	*Le Monde*	*Jerusalem Post*	*al-Ahram*
New York Times (city)	1.0					
New York Times (late)	.97	1.0				
Times (London)	.93	.86	1.0			
Le Monde	.92	.91	.89	1.0		
Jerusalem Post	.97	.92	.97	.92	1.0	
al-Ahram	.97	.94	.95	.90	.99	1.0

The rank-order correlations for similarities in attention level to actors are reported in Table I-8.

For purposes of analysis, the categories thus far used are too gross for testing hypotheses developed in the literature on international conflict and crisis. One hypothesis developed from the earlier studies of the 1914 crisis is that decision makers under stress view their own nations as the victim of hostile environments in which their efforts to conduct peaceful policies go unreciprocated. As a measure of this notion of unrequited friendship, Holsti, and North (1965) developed the following measure:

$$\frac{\text{Units of friendship as agent}}{\text{Units of friendship as target}}$$

As the ratio increases above one, the perceiver sees himself as the author of friendly moves which are not reciprocated. Holsti and North added to this the concept of the perceiver as victim of a hostile environment of which he is primarily a target and not an agent. This is expressed as follows:

$$\frac{\text{Units of hostility as target}}{\text{Units of hostility as agent}}$$

Again, as the ratio increases above one, the perceiver sees himself increasingly as the victim of a hostile environment. The two measures were combined to form what was first called an index of paranoia and subsequently redefined (Holsti and Hopmann, 1966) as an index of injury:

$$\frac{\text{Units of friendship as agent plus units of hostility as target}}{\text{Units of friendship as target plus units of hostility as agent}}$$

TABLE I-7

COVERAGE OF PRINCIPAL ACTORS' EXTERNAL RELATIONS IN ELITE PRESS (May 1967)

Actors	*New York Times* (early) Items n	Rank	*New York Times* (late) Items n	Rank	*Times* (London) Items n	Rank	*Le Monde* (Paris) Items n	Rank	*Jerusalem Post* Items n	Rank	*al-Ahram* Items n	Rank
USA	152	(1)	155	(1)	76	(2)	65	(1)	118	(3)	169	(2)
UNK	72	(3)	62	(4)	109	(1)	51	(2)	55	(6)	102	(4)
FRN	24	(8)	22	(8)	10	(8)	24	(8)	36	(7)	27	(7)
USR	63	(4.5)	44	(6)	51	(4)	34	(4)	76	(4)	74	(5)
UNO	40	(7)	42	(7)	32	(7)	30	(5)	73	(5)	63	(6)
UAR	91	(2)	74	(3)	74	(3)	50	(3)	165	(2)	447	(1)
ISR	63	(4.5)	82	(2)	40	(5)	25	(7)	206	(1)	107	(3)
CHN	56	(6)	48	(5)	35	(6)	27	(6)	22	(8)	15	(8)
Totals	561		529		427		306		751		1,004	

TABLE I-8
RANK-ORDER CORRELATIONS IN COVERAGE OF PRINCIPAL ACTORS IN THE ELITE PRESS (May 1967)

Regions	*New York Times* (early)	*New York Times* (late)	*Times* (London)	*Le Monde*	*Jerusalem Post*	*al-Ahram*
New York Times (eity)	1.0					
New York Times (late)	.87	1.0				
Times (London)	.92	.72	1.0			
Le Monde	.85	.55	.88	1.0		
Jerusalem Post	.59	.66	.38	.26	1.0	
al-Ahram	.88	.79	.69	.60	.86	1.0

The Stanford studies used this index with weighted data derived from the semantic differential analysis of elite perceptions. Here we employ the index using only the frequency of event data and a simple hostility-friendship dichotomy based on a collapsing of the WEIS categories suggested by Moore and Young (1969). The friendship category is formed by collapsing the following WEIS categories: yield, grant, reward, approve, promise, agree, request and propose. The hostility category is created by collapsing the following categories: reject, accuse, protest, deny, demand, warn, threaten, demonstrate, reduce relationship, expel, seize and force. The comment and consult categories are dropped from the analysis as "neutral" on the friendship-hostility dimension.[8] This collapsing of categories could incidentally be expected to result in substantially higher intercoder reliability but at a price of considerable blurring of the distinctions between various types of foreign policy actions. It should also be noted that the hypothesis on perception was based on the notion that decision makers under stress would be subject to considerable cognitive distortion. We are attempting to explore the notion that reporters and gatekeepers of international news flow, while not subject to the same degree of stress as the decision makers, may also differ, due to their own national and other biases, in their reports of which nations appear as victims or agents of hostile environments.

The index can be computed using specific bilateral channels, e.g., the United States (USA) and the Soviet Union (USSR), or on the basis of the total output and input of a specific actor with his external environment, e.g., the foreign policy profile of the United States. We have first computed the index of injury for the foreign policy profiles of seven principal actors (Table I-9).[9] The reader should note that the foreign

TABLE I-9

INDEX OF INJURY (May 1967)

	(1) Agent Positive	(2) Target Positive	(3) Agent Negative	(4) Target Negative	(1) + (4) / (2) + (3)
New York Times (city)					
USA	29	12	21	44	2.21
UNK	6	5	8	24	2.30
USR	7	6	21	9	.59
UNO	3	11	2	6	.69
UAR	11	15	24	14	.64
ISR	4	4	12	18	1.37
CHN	1	1	27	18	.68
New York Times (late)					
USA	22	16	20	41	1.75
UNK	4	7	9	22	1.63
USR	2	6	12	13	.83
UNO	6	12	4	1	.44
UAR	10	13	25	9	.50
ISR	3	6	14	33	1.80
CHN	3	0	28	9	.43
Times (London)					
USA	11	5	12	23	1.55
UNK	16	13	18	27	1.39
USR	9	7	13	7	.80
UNO	4	9	4	2	.46
UAR	6	6	23	18	.83
ISR	2	1	5	23	4.17
CHN	2	0	23	6	.35
Le Monde					
USA	10	12	5	16	1.53
UNK	8	10	5	10	1.20
USR	11	2	10	6	1.42
UNO	4	11	2	1	.38
UAR	3	8	10	2	.28
ISR	0	4	4	9	1.13
CHN	2	2	19	3	.24
Jerusalem Post					
USA	22	7	15	31	2.41
UNK	7	7	15	14	.95
USR	12	7	24	9	.68
UNO	11	12	6	11	.79
UAR	19	21	51	16	.49
ISR	14	26	36	74	1.42
CHN	2	1	13	4	.36
al-Ahram					
USA	24	14	26	50	1.85
UNK	12	9	15	27	1.62
USR	11	8	10	4	.83
UNO	9	16	5	8	.80
UAR	53	60	39	21	.74
ISR	8	14	26	30	.95
CHN	2	2	8	2	.40

policy profiles only tell us what the overall position of the actor was in an international system. Different sources might agree on the profile but have quite different distributions of these outputs and inputs according to target and source.

Using first the distinction between victim of injury and agent of injury (above and below 1.0 respectively), we find substantial agreement among our sources. The *Jerusalem Post* differs from the others in seeing the United Kingdom (UNK) as more agent than victim of a hostile environment. *Le Monde* differs in seeing the Soviet Union as more victim than agent of a hostile environment. *Al-Ahram* differs in seeing Israel as more agent than victim of a hostile environment, but even here Israel is less the agent of hostility than the UAR which preserves the same rank order as the others. The *Times* (London) sees Israel as much more the victim of injury than the others. Similarities as measured by rank order correlations are reported in Table I-10.

The *New York Times* (city edition) generally correlated less well with the others because of the difference in the relative ranking of the Soviet Union which appeared in the WEIS data as the highest ranking agent of hostility. *Le Monde* on the other hand reported the Soviet Union as the next most injured party after the United States. The low correlation between these two sources largely reflects the differences in treatment of the Soviet Union.

As a final comparison, we constructed the index of injury on two bilateral channels—the United States-Soviet Union and the UAR-Israel. The results are reported in Table I-11. A principal difficulty with event data of this type emerges here in the small number of events that can be isolated by channel, even when aggregating over a one-month period for

TABLE I-10

RANK-ORDER CORRELATIONS IN INDEX OF INJURY IN ELITE PRESS (May 1967)

Regions	*New York Times* (city)	*New York Times* (late)	*Times* (London)	*Le Monde*	*Jerusalem Post*	*al-Ahram*
New York Times (city)	1.0					
New York Times (late)	.54	1.0				
Times (London)	.57	.96	1.0			
Le Monde	.36	.71	.57	1.0		
Jerusalem Post	.75	.86	.82	.75	1.0	
al-Ahram	.71	.87	.79	.89	.93	1.0

TABLE I-11
INDEX OF INJURY IN PRINCIPAL BILATERAL RELATIONS IN THE ELITE PRESS (May 1967)

	(1) Agent Positive	(2) Target Positive	(3) Agent Negative	(4) Target Negative	(1) + (4) / (2) + (3)
USA to USR					
New York Times (city)	2	0	5	12	2.80
New York Times (late)	2	0	3	7	3.00
Times (London)	1	0	0	4	0
Le Monde	0	1	1	2	1.00
Jerusalem Post	3	2	4	8	1.83
al-Ahram	1	2	3	3	.80
UAR to ISR					
New York Times (city)	0	1	5	8	1.33
New York Times (late)	0	1	14	7	.47
Times (London)	0	0	8	4	.50
Le Monde	0	0	6	1	.17
Jerusalem Post	0	0	16	7	.44
al-Ahram	0	0	9	13	1.44

major protagonists during an intense international crisis. Because our ratios are based on very small frequencies, coder differences in selection and categorization of events could be quite critical in the construction of indices. For example, the WEIS data unlike the other three Western sources and the Israeli press show Egypt as the target of greater Israeli hostility. How can we account for this striking difference? Do the two editions of the *New York Times* differ on this point in their reporting? The question of intercoder reliability in this instance is critical if we are to make comparisons across sources. As it stands, we have no way of knowing whether or not we are comparing differing source coverage or differing judgments by coders or what combination of the two. Unless this problem can be resolved, users of event data should be careful in their interpretations of what are presumed to be substantive findings about either sources or international system behavior as reported in those sources. For crisis analysis, we may need to take extraordinary pains in generating sufficient data for quantitative analysis as well as quality control on the data generated.

The thinness of our data appears to be a reflection of the narrow criteria by which a relevant intergovernmental event was defined in the WEIS system. Considerable contextual information has been lost. By concentrating only on intergovernmental actions, we have eliminated a great deal of reported information about within-nation decision processes and influences which bear upon the international situation. Much of the activity reported, particularly in *al-Ahram,* was concerned with internation consultations which were eliminated from the friendship-hostility categories. A first impression, subject to further analysis, is that the Arab-Israeli crisis of 1967 was characterized by an extraordinary amount of within-coalition consultation with very little attention to between-coalition bargaining. This was one of the findings of the 1914 study which merits considerably greater study with regard to 1967 and other crises.

Substantively, the index of injury comparison in Table 11 suggests that events themselves are quite differently perceived. The Western sources and the Israeli source all agree that the United States was the relative victim in the few Soviet-American interactions in the month. Four of these sources see Israel as the victim in the Egyptian-Israeli interaction pattern. *Al-Ahram* reports the opposite: Egypt and its ally, the Soviet Union, were each victims in the interactions with their principal protagonists. If we are to use event data sources—despite their reputations for objectivity—from only one side of a controversy, do we not bias our conclusions? If we aggregate data from multiple sources as has been done by a number of writers who recognize the problem of differential coverage, then we may throw away valuable material to test hypotheses about differences in the basic definition of the situation as a principal ingredient in internation conflict. The events data analyst may be able to extend further the work of the Stanford group on elite perceptions and misperceptions in exploring a fundamental notion put forward by Wright (1965: 1503):

> Subjective illusions, false images of the world, disparity between the "self-image" and the "other-image" of nations have never been more influential in the beliefs of people and the policies of governments. Inter-national relations is concerned less with the relations between nations than with relations between false images of nations.

CONCLUSIONS

Several methodological and substantive problems have been raised in the course of this study. The first has to do with the question of microcosmic measures of intercoder reliability in generating events data from sources which contain a large number of stimuli, such as coding intergovernmental actions from the full coverage of the *New York Times.* While we should continue to strive for improved reliability by clearer definition of categories, the use of more than one coder in covering the original source material, and more intensive training of coders, we should also recognize that the high levels of intercoder reliability associated with the coding of open-ended responses on surveys are not likely to be obtained with this type of event data. The generators of event data should be much clearer in reporting full reliability tests so users can be clearer about the limitations of the data. One solution to the problem of reliability might be the use of a preselected chronology such as that found in the *New York Times Index* or *Keesing's Contemporary Archives*.. The problem is not really removed, for the decision on what to code has been made by the preparers of the chronology by generally unknown criteria. The planned computerized *New York Times Index* may help alleviate the problem in that computers are more reliable and accurate in such tedious and iterative tasks as are involved in content analysis.

The use of global sources will nevertheless not be satisfactory for the analysis of events between more peripheral members of the international system. Use of sources specializing in regional material will be necessary; the much more intensive coverage of the Middle East by the *Jerusalem Post* and *al-Ahram* is quite clear from our presentation. The use of chronologies which are derived from area newspapers and other sources may be one answer to the problem of objectivity. Burrowes' (1969) use of the *Cahiers de l'Orient Contemporain* bears out the merit of this approach to regional questions. Differential coverage of events data may itself be an important subject for inquiry, however. One solution to the problem of selection of events from many pages of newsprint is to use only front-page headline analysis. This approach has the additional merit of providing some greater measure of saliency of events to elites than the coding of the entire newspaper where small "fillers" are accorded the same weight as major items on the front page. Even here there are problems, however, in that *al-Ahram* has about twice as many items on the front page as the *Jerusalem Post*. Conclusions based on the relative complexity of the imagery of Egyptian gatekeepers relative to that of the Israelis would be based on a comparison of quite different size samples.

In raising some of the many problems associated with the generation and analysis of events data, we do intend to encourage more effort by a larger number of people. An important objective in this exercise was the training of a number of political science students, graduate and undergraduate, in the problems of data generation and analysis in the social sciences. Our overall conclusion is that this has been a far more creative exercise than the memorization of jargon or the passive role of reading and commenting upon recent articles in international relations research. Events data generation and analysis raises one of the most promising subjects for the creation on a global basis of the societal observatories which Lasswell (1963) envisaged for the future of a truly international and policy-relevant political science.

NOTES

1. In the early codebook, Martin and Young (1968) indicated that they would use Scott's (1955) pi and Funkhouser and Parker's (1968) random systematic error coefficient in calculating intercoder reliability. It is not entirely clear in the McClelland and Hoggard (1969) article how the .83 intercoder reliability coefficient for the 1966 WEIS data was calculated.

2. The two-edition differential coverage phenomenon is apparently not well known in Washington either. Vice President Agnew accused the *New York Times* of bias by failing to report a major news story on congressmen who signed a statement supporting the President's policy on Vietnam (see the *New York Times* of November 22, 1969). The day following the charge, *Times* president and publisher Arthur Ochs Sulzberger pointed out that the story had been carried prominently in the late city edition of the *Times* but not in the one which is circulated in Washington. This anecdote suggests that differences in coverage between the two editions are not entirely trivial. Whether or not the late city edition (the one on microfilm) is more comprehensive is a matter for more investigation. Our research is certainly not conclusive on this point.

3. Janda (1968: 43) reports similar problems in reliability with pretests of information retrieval on party politics with coding reliabilities of .50 and .47 for substantive information, substantially below the .8 and .9 reliabilities achieved in coding open-ended responses on surveys. The larger number of coding categories and the fact that each page presents many stimuli to the coder accounts for the lower reliabilities associated with this form of content analysis.

4. In some early months of the WEIS collection—including the period covered here—only one coder covered the material initially with reliability checks performed on the assignment of categories. Once the WEIS project was fully under way after January 1968, more than one coder had covered the same material in order to guard against the selective omission problem suggested here. The WEIS coders have now recoded the Middle East war period, but we have not been able as yet to compare the results of the revised WEIS file with the file reported here to see if there is significant improvement. The revised file contains considerably more items than the original. As our replication was already on the low side in comparison with the more experienced WEIS coders, the gap should be even wider with the problems residing largely in the inadequate training of our coders.

5. For other approaches to the resolution of this problem in event data generation, consult McGowan (1971).

6. The use of the product-moment correlation shows substantially reduced correlation of *al-Ahram* and the *Jerusalem Post* with the other newspapers because of the presence of very large deviations in the Middle East category. "Similarity" is not an unambiguous notion, and the researcher should be clear in reporting his results that there may be substantial differences according to the test used. In this sense, *al-Ahram* and the *Jerusalem Post* are far richer sources of data on the Middle East in this month and therefore quite dissimilar on this point from the other sources used.

7. The choice of "principal actors" was made on the basis of the research design—the great powers, the UN, and the principal area protagonists—and not on the

basis of the actual rank orders of coverage in each of the newspapers. Again, one should note the ambiguity of the concept of "similarity." "Actor" is also somewhat ambiguous in the sense that these scores were obtained by including all items in which the particular unit is reported, both as actor and as target.

8. Calhoun (1971) used judges to scale the 22 WEIS categories and factor-analyzed their responses to create a two-dimensional interval scale of the WEIS categories. The "consult" category emerged as the second most cooperative category rather than neutral as used here.

9. France was eliminated from the list due to insufficient reporting across the sources used.

REFERENCES

AZAR, E., T. JUKAM, J. McCORMICK, and S. COHEN (1969) "A quantitative comparison of source coverage for events data: preliminary findings." Michigan State University Department of Political Science. (mimeo)

BURROWES, R. (1969) "The strength and direction of relationships between domestic and external conflict: Syria, 1961-67." New York University Department of Political Science. (mimeo)

CALHOUN, H. (1971) "The measurement and scaling of event data using the semantic differential." University of Southern California World Event Interaction Survey Project. (mimeo)

CORSON, W. H. (1969) "Measuring conflict and cooperation intensity in international relations." Harvard University. (mimeo)

FUNKHOUSER, G. R. and E. B. PARKER (1968) "Analyzing coding reliability: the random-systematic-error coefficient." Public Opinion Q. 32 (Spring): 122-128.

GALTUNG, J. and M. H. RUGE (1965) "The structure of foreign news: the presentation of the Congo, Cuba, and Cyprus crises in four Norwegian newspapers." J. of Peace Research 2, 1: 64-91.

HOGGARD, G. D. (1967) "Comparison of reporting for the New York Times Index, Asian Recorder, and deadline data–Chinese interactions January through October, 1962." University of Southern California World Event Interaction Survey Project. (mimeo)

HOLSTI, O. R. and P. T. HOPMANN (1966) "Israeli and Egyptian attitudes: October-November, 1956." Stanford University Institute of Political Studies. Studies in International Conflict and Integration. (mimeo)

HOLSTI, O. R. and R. C. NORTH (1965) "History as a laboratory of conflict," pp. 155-171 in E. B. McNeil (ed.) The Nature of Human Conflict. Englewood Cliffs, N.J.: Prentice-Hall.

HOLSTI, O. R., R. A. BRODY, and R. C. NORTH (1964) "Measuring affect and action in international reaction models: empirical materials from the 1962 Cuban missile crisis." Papers of Peace Research Society (International) 2: 170-190.

JANDA, K. (1969) "A microfilm and computer system for analyzing comparative political literature," pp. 407-436 in G. Gerbner (ed.) The Analysis of Communication Content. New York: John Wiley.

--- (1968) Information Retrieval. Indianapolis: Bobbs-Merrill.

JERVIS, R. (1967) "The costs of the scientific study of politics: an examination of the Stanford content analysis studies." International Studies Q. 11 (December): 366-393.

LASSWELL, H. D. (1963) The Future of Political Science. New York: Atherton.
MARTIN, W. R. and R. A. YOUNG (1968) "World event interaction survey (WEIS) program: rules and instructions." University of Southern California. (mimeo)
McCLELLAND, C. A. (1969) "Working papers of the WEIS project." University of Southern California World Event Interaction Survey Project. (mimeo)
--- and G. D. HOGGARD (1969) "Conflict patterns in the interactions among nations," pp. 711-724 in J. N. Rosenau (ed.) International Politics and Foreign Policy. New York: Free Press.
McGOWAN, P. J. (1971) "A Bayesian approach to the problem of events data validity in comparative and international political research." Syracuse University Department of Political Science. (mimeo)
MOORE, J. A. and R. A. YOUNG (1969) "Some preliminary short-term predictions of international interaction." University of Southern California World Event Interaction Survey Project. (mimeo)
MOSES, L. E., R. A. BRODY, O. R. HOLSTI, J. B. KADANE, and J. S. MILSTEIN (1967) "Scaling data on inter-nation action." Science 156 (May 26): 1054-1059.
NORTH, R. C., O. R. HOLSTI, G. ZANINOVITCH, and D. A. ZINNES (1963) Content Analysis: A Handbook with Applications for the Study of International Crisis. Evanston, Ill.: Northwestern Univ. Press.
POOL, I. D. [ed.] (1959) Trends in Content Analysis. Urbana, Ill.: Univ. of Illinois Press.
SCOTT, W. A. (1955) "Reliability of content analysis: the case of nominal scale coding." Public Opinion Q. 19 (Winter): 321-325.
SMITH, R. F. (1969) "On the structure of foreign news: a comparison of the New York Times and the Indian White Papers." J. of Peace Research 6, 1: 23-26.
WRIGHT, Q. (1965) A Study of War. Chicago: Univ. of Chicago Press.

Chapter II

THE SINO-INDIAN BORDER CONFLICT: AN EXPLORATORY ANALYSIS OF ACTION AND PERCEPTION

John Osgood Field
with the assistance of
Nazli Choucri and William C. Mitchell

The advantages and shortcomings of quantitative research in the study of international politics are well recognized by now. While precision and systematic analysis are sometimes promoted at the expense of realism and gut politics, the resulting imbalance stems less from the limitations of methodology than from our inability as yet to bring quantitative modes of analysis to bear sufficiently upon investigations of political events. All too often the gap between technique and substance is so wide as to preclude the effective linkage of precision with politics.

AUTHOR'S NOTE: *An earlier version of this chapter was presented as a paper at the Events Data Conference, Michigan State University, East Lansing, during the period February 28 to March 2, 1969, organized and chaired by Edward E. Azar. For helpful comments and criticism at various stages in the paper's preparation, the authors would like to thank Ole R. Holsti, Richard A. Brody, J. David Singer, Robert C. North, Paul Smoker and an anonymous reviewer. The operational assistance of Mr. Kuan Lee is gratefully acknowledged, as is the use of the computer facilities at Stanford University.*

The analysis reported in this paper represents an attempt to bridge this gap separating method and realism. Substantively, we are interested in the interaction of states in situations of tension, hostility and profound instability. The methodological questions of concern to us relate to the measurement and analysis both of nation-state behavior and of the perceptual orientations of national leaderships seeking to cope with crisis events. At issue is how perceptions influence actions when two states are locked in conflict.

This study is exploratory in nature. It is essentially an experiment with novel empirical tools. We are not at all satisfied with the outcome of our work; nor are we prepared to defend every research decision we have made. On the other hand, it is clear to us that significant advances in the quantitative analysis of international politics will occur only after considerable experimentation. This study is one such effort on a long and difficult, often frustrating, road.

ACTION AND PERCEPTION IN CONFLICT SITUATIONS

The central objective of our research has been to isolate the determinants of behavior when two states are in armed conflict. We have sought to examine systematically the relationship between perceptions and actions—between what is thought and what is done—in a highly charged atmosphere characterized by actual combat. The historical case in question is the Sino-Indian border dispute of 1962, specifically those twelve days at the end of October which featured bitter fighting.[1] Our analysis is based on documentary data, processed via automated content analysis, and behavioral data, scaled according to levels of violence. The problem before us is to relate perceptions and actions and to identify linkages between them.

Perceptions are definitions of reality and for this reason assume major significance in orienting behavior. As Kenneth Boulding (1959: 123) has noted, "Nations do not respond to the 'objective' facts of the situation but to their image of the situation." This is fine as a general principle, if only as a reminder that people make the decisions which commit nation-states and that the perceptions of decision makers may differ markedly under similar, even identical circumstances. What is not well understood, however, is how latitude for interpretation changes from one kind of interaction to another. Is it not possible for a situation to be so compelling as to produce an almost automatic response? This is the question to which our study is addressed.

In examining this question systematically we have utilized an interaction model developed by the Stanford Studies in International Conflict and Integration. The model is designed to determine the impact of perceptions on actual behavior in dyadic or multiple relationships. It is based on the well-known concepts of "stimulus" and "response," representing sets of actions linked by a two-step mediation process. Stated simply, the model (depicted as S–r : s–R) suggests that, upon becoming aware of an external event, individuals, groups or nations size up the problem, calculate their interests and then react. The two intervening steps are (1) perception of external stimuli and (2) formulation of one's own position. Together these assessments relate sets of mutually directed behavior (Holsti et al., 1964a). When applied to international politics this model can be defined as follows:

- S: is an "objective" event in the environment coming to the attention of a state's decision makers and stimulating some sort of response (including conceivably inaction).
- r: represents perception of the stimulus by the decision makers. It is, in essence, their definition of the situation as revealed by their speeches, public statements and diplomatic messages.
- s: is the decision makers' assertion of their own attitude and intent in handling the stimulus or in dealing with its source (most likely another state). It is derived from the same materials as r.
- R: stands for the "objective" response or behavior of the state.

This model, along with the relationships it seeks to describe, is a highly simplified representation of reality, so much so that the charge of oversimplification (if not outright distortion) may be raised. Yet simplification is sometimes mistaken for parsimony. The real question in research of this kind is whether one gets at the essence of a situation by structuring it in such a fashion, or whether the model and methods employed merely obscure reality in a pile of numbers largely devoid of meaning.

In formulating our research we decided that the components of the interaction model would be useful for purposes of ordering the data and for relating different types of information to each other. We felt that the distinctions among external stimuli, perceptions of those stimuli, plans or intentions with regard to the situation at hand, and overt behavior would enable us to decompose the interaction process and untangle various strands of it sufficiently to apply systematic modes of investigation and bring a semblance of order to an otherwise confusing array of data. Moreover, these distinctions allow us to consider explicit hypotheses concerning "automatic" reaction processes as opposed to mediated reaction processes, all of which may be submitted to empirical testing.

In a dyadic relationship, such as that between India and China, one state's action may be a stimulus for the other. If the interaction is closely knit, as in the border conflict it definitely was, mutually oriented attention and behavior will be especially pronounced. Consequently, Sino-Indian relations during October 1962 may be depicted as follows:

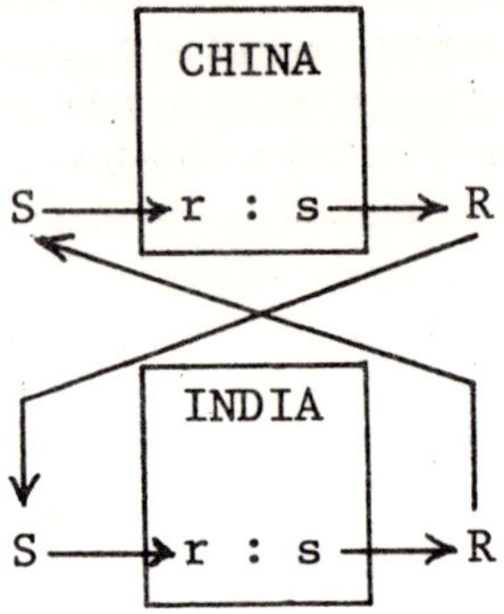

China's behavior is said to stimulate some type of response by India, after perceptual mediation, and this response in turn enters the Chinese system, influencing its behavior in an ongoing series of interactions.

A major question in any such interaction concerns which antecedent variable (S, r or s) is the best predictor of a state's response (R). Another way of putting this would be to ask under what conditions perceptions modify responsive behavior from what would be predicted solely by reference to the stimulus. The findings of several case studies suggest that, indeed, states respond less to objective events than to their perceptions of these events and conclusions drawn from them. For example, it has been argued that consistency between action and reaction will be higher in low-reward, low-penalty situations than otherwise, but that the more negatively involved the relations between two states become—up to a certain threshold—the more likely will their respective definitions of the situation (r) determine their behavior (North, 1964). There is empirical evidence to suggest that in extremely negative contexts a state's declared intent (s) correlates best with its overt behavior (R). This relationship is essentially one of mistranslation or misperception resulting from the distorting effects of high stress (Zaninovitch, 1964). Either way, perceptual mediation is believed to be of greater significance in tense situations than when interaction is peaceful, routine or of minor importance.

The principal hypothesis of this paper asserts a ceiling or upper level above which perceptions become less relevant to behavioral response than actual stimuli. Just where this ceiling is—if it exists at all—a single study obviously cannot determine; but the decisive factor might be the existence of open, armed hostilities. When a challenge is both unambiguously visible and serious, the importance of subjective evaluation is likely to be reduced. The decision makers of a country, faced with armed confrontation, may have little margin for calculating an appropriate response, either in the sense of attributing meaning to the events or in deciding what to do about them. Violence begets violence quite automatically under these conditions, we would suggest. With little latitude for interpretation, perceptions simply define what is obvious and orient as is necessary. They become tactically supportive, indicating how to respond as one must.[2]

Whereas most studies utilizing this conceptual framework have dealt with events leading to the outbreak of violence (as in 1914 and the Suez crisis of 1956) or with events featuring a conflict spiral which turned downward prior to and precluding an outbreak (as in the Cuban missile crisis), this study is concerned with a period in which two states fall quite suddenly and dramatically into a state of belligerence. The border dispute, therefore, offers a promising case with which to test this hypothesis; and it permits us to probe the nexus between perceptions and behavior in a situation characterized by reasonably high intensities of violence.

Methodologically, the border conflict lends itself to an attempt to relate actions and perceptions systematically. Such an effort is long overdue. The overwhelming emphasis in the literature to date has centered either on events, actions and interactions, or on perceptions, attitudes and dispositions. Few studies in recent years have sought to join these two foci in anything resembling rigorous fashion (but see Holsti et al., 1964b). We are making an attempt to do so here.

THE SINO-INDIAN BORDER DISPUTE[3]

Contrary to public conception, Sino-Indian relations have been characterized by a fairly high degree of tension ever since the People's Republic was proclaimed in 1949. During the early years the Chinese did not hesitate to denounce Indian Prime Minister Nehru as a "running dog of imperialism"; and while, on the surface, the hard line gave way in 1954 to a spirit of Panchshila,[4] important questions remained unsolved.

The most persistent of these problems concerned the demarcation of their mutual frontier, the longest shared by any Communist with a non-Communist state (2,500 miles). Throughout the 1950s the Indian government politely accused the Chinese of cartographic aggression. The standard reply was that maps being printed in China were reproductions of those published under the Kuomintang and that the necessary adjustments would be made as soon as the new regime had the time to do so. But early in 1959, after India had disclosed its discovery of a Chinese road running through eastern Ladakh, Peking laid claim to the entire area contained in the Kuomintang maps, over 50,000 square miles.

The Tibetan revolt soon after caused a further deterioration in relations, as India granted diplomatic asylum to the Dalai Lama and more than 12,000 Tibetan refugees. Subsequent negotiations to settle the border issue, including a visit by Premier Chou En-lai to New Delhi in 1960, all failed; and mutual charges of troop incursions and violations of air space became increasingly bitter. In November 1961, Prime Minister Nehru declared that India would continue to strengthen its border forces until "we may be in a position to recover such territory as is now in the possession of the Chinese."

Minor conflicts broke out in July 1962, accompanied by strongly worded protests from both sides. On September 8 the level of tension rose appreciably as a unit of approximately 200 Chinese troops crossed the Himalayan watershed (McMahon Line) and entered disputed territory in India's North-East Frontier Agency. Peking simultaneously called for new border talks to be held without setting preconditions. This India rejected, stipulating that the Chinese Government must first take concrete measures to undo its infringement of Indian territory. On October 5 the Indian government announced the formation of a special Frontier Corps, prompting China to accuse it of spreading "the flames of war." A week later Nehru revealed that the government had ordered the Indian army to remove Chinese forces from Indian soil, by force if necessary. Peking responded with warnings of dire consequences should this be attempted, and reports of large-scale Chinese buildups along the frontier began to reach New Delhi near the middle of the month. At the same time, sources in China stressed the threat of a "massive Indian offensive."

Early in the morning of October 20, 1962, the roof fell in. Each side accused the other of initiating major hostilities in both Ladakh and the North-East Frontier Agency (NEFA).[5] The facts would seem to be that Chinese troops, estimated at 20,000 strong, attacked eleven of sixteen Indian military outposts in northern Ladakh (four of which fell), two others in southern Ladakh (one, possibly both, fell), and undertook a two-pronged invasion south of the McMahon line in NEFA, forcing Indian units back as much as four miles in rugged mountain country. Reports reaching New Delhi said that the Chinese attacked in waves, as in Korea, armed with medium machine guns and supported by heavy mortars.

The contest was conspicuously one-sided. China's well-equipped troops opened new fronts repeatedly and overran almost every Indian frontier post from the Burmese border in the east to northern Ladakh in the west. Indian supply planes were shot down, as were helicopters evacuating the wounded. India's foot soldiers were outnumbered, poorly clothed for the Himalayas, and—until arms arrived from the United States and Britain—often reliant on World War I Royal Enfield rifles. On October 29, the government admitted having lost "thousands" of men in the fighting and 5,000 square miles in addition to the 12,000 previously occupied by the Chinese. Two days later Prime Minister Nehru dismissed his close confidant V. K. Krishna Menon as Minister of Defense, assuming that portfolio himself. It might be noted, however, that three of India's better divisions in Kashmir were kept on the Pakistan side because of the chronic tensions there.

Diplomatically, the frequent exchanges between the two capitals continued. Peking proposed settling the conflict on the basis of (1) a cease fire, (2) mutual withdrawal of troops 20 kilometers behind the "line of actual control" and (3) high-level talks. New Delhi, conscious of the fact that this "line of actual control" was changing each day in China's favor, insisted that Chinese troops return to their positions of September 8 as a precondition for negotiations. The Indian government made every effort to keep the Soviet Union at least benevolently neutral (with considerable success); and on October 29, in a sharp break with past policy, a formal request for military assistance was sent to the United States. By contrast, the People's Republic proclaimed itself self-sufficient in repelling Indian "aggression" and neither asked for nor received aid.

On the domestic front, little information is available regarding China. In India economic planning was revised for defense spending in anticipation of a long struggle.[6] Civil defense measures were introduced, and national air service was sharply cut to release pilots for war duty. On October 26 President Radhakrishnan declared a state of national emergency, giving the government almost unlimited powers. Elections were postponed, ceremonies and sporting events cancelled, and naturalized Chinese residents first restricted in their movements and then stripped of citizenship.

A more complete study would have to relate both India and China to their domestic and international environments with greater precision. As far as the political and strategic ramifications of the crisis are concerned, a definite injustice is committed by treating the two countries in dyadic isolation. Figure II-1 is offered to offset this limitation somewhat. Fortunately, the testing of our hypothesis is not adversely affected by excluding other states from consideration.

Stating our inquiry in terms of the border dispute, we are asking whether Chinese and Indian behaviors were predicated most directly on

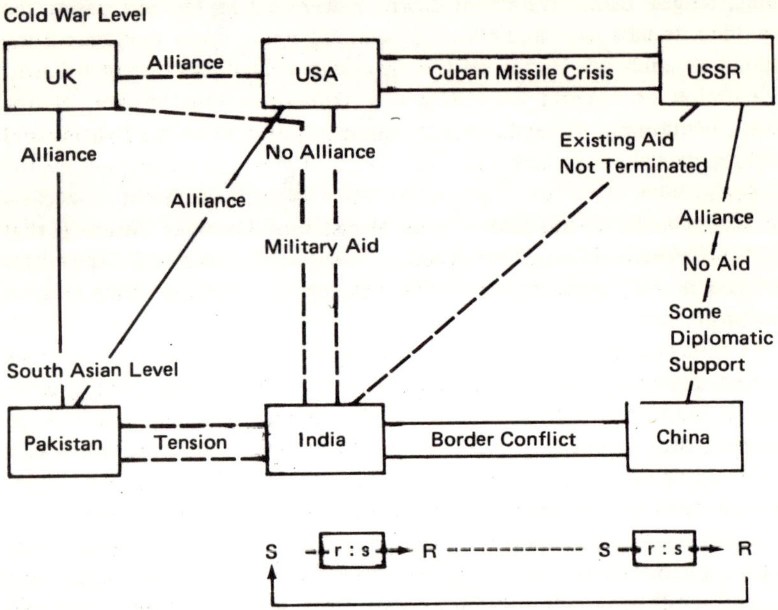

Figure II-1: THE SINO-INDIAN CONFLICT IN SYSTEMIC CONTEXT OCTOBER 20-31, 1962

each other's actions or on perceptions of the other and oneself. The following sections present perceptual and behavioral data and will examine their interrelation.

PERCEPTUAL DATA: CONTENT ANALYSIS OF POLITICAL DOCUMENTS

In this section we examine Indian and Chinese perceptions during the period of October 22-31, 1962. Our purpose is to assess each country's evaluations of itself and its adversary and in so doing to report data which may be compared subsequently with scaled behavior. Perceptions are inferred from the content of official statements released by both countries in domestic broadcasts, formal memoranda, diplomatic notes, and the like. Statements by the Indian leadership were relatively easy to come by, whereas Chinese documents were less readily available.

It is important to emphasize that by relying on the written record we are in fact tapping expressed attitudes. Whether official expressions of sentiment reflect actual perception of a situation is one of those nagging questions which cannot be answered definitively in this instance. We have been obliged to treat them as such; and while we do not claim that perceptions inferred from official materials are in some way metaphysically true, they are a rich source of information concerning the formal orientation of national leaderships and their positions on the issues at hand. Tentatively, at least, we were prepared to accept the equivalence of statements and perceptions.

Perceptions of events (r) and each state's own assessment of its position (s) are recorded by the General Inquirer system of content analysis (Holsti et al., 1964a; Stone, 1966; Holsti, 1968) on the basis of three basic dimensions of perceptual orientation: affect, potency and activity. Extensive cross-cultural analysis has established that social perceptions tend to crystallize around these three dimensions, on the basis of which further cognitive structuring is then erected (Osgood et al., 1957). In the case of the Sino-Indian border dispute we can assume that when two states interact, each perceives the other and itself in these terms. Affect refers to positive and negative orientations, potency entails perceptions of strength and weakness and activity denotes activity and passivity.

Operationally, the General Inquirer system consists of a dictionary applying values to substantive words according to these dimensions. In the version which we used, the dictionary provides gradations of sentiment for each dimension across a seven-point scale, from very positive (+3) to very negative (–3)–or strong and weak, or active and passive–with a point of perceptual neutrality (0) separating the two directional signs of the scale. The seven-point scale brings out the intensity of feeling, while the frequency of expression can be said to tap the degree of salience of the attitude in question. The combination of frequency and intensity provides insight into each actor's cognitive and affective framework concerning other actors and itself.

Although some questions might be raised concerning the comparability of Chinese and Indian documents, several pertinent results deserve mention.[7] With reference to Chinese and Indian perceptions of each other and themselves, our data indicate that both countries in their public pronouncements between October 22 and 31 consistently perceived the other as the more hostile. China tended to regard India as stronger and itself as weaker, a rather startling finding, while India's perceptions fluctuated, no doubt inspired by promises of aid from the West and a few minor victories in the last three days of the month. The two states differed sharply in their perceptions along the activity dimension. China saw India as the more active until October 28 and considered itself as the more passive throughout. India likewise perceived itself as the more passive and also credited China with greater activity until October 31, when in fact Indian troops appeared temporarily to have taken the initiative.

While the findings for India seem reasonable enough, those with respect to China's perceptions of itself as less negative, strong, and active are intriguing, to ay the least. Such findings certainly indicate considerable discrepancy between perceived and objective conditions. The problem may lie in the selection of coded documents. The only Chinese statements available for consideration were those released by the government for public consumption, and there may have been a deliberate effort at falsification designed to camouflage a premeditated attack on India. As Prime Minister Nehru (1962: 19) commented at the time:

> The way the Chinese put it is to appear as meek lambs being devoured by tigers from India from which they had to defend themselves. It is quite extraordinary that the meek lamb goes on devouring our territory.

Unfortunately, methods have not been devised to determine whether this was in fact the case, but it is possible.

On the other hand, we know from previous empirical analyses that it is not uncommon for actors engaged in conflict to perceive opponents as more hostile, more powerful and more active than they perceive themselves to be (Holsti, 1965). Public posturing aside, extensive theoretical work on sources of misperception, irrational assessments and cognitive distortion provide sufficient basis for the possibility of such an eventuality in this instance (Jervis, 1967 and 1968; Verba, 1961; de Rivera 1968).

To some extent, the uncertainty regarding the genuineness of Chinese perceptions may be narrowed if, contrary to our hypothesis, those perceptions are good predictors of China's actions in the border war. Of course, if they are not good predictors, we will not know whether this is because they were deliberately misleading or because they had little independent effect. At any rate, by relating the perceptions of both states to their actions it should be possible to gain more insight into the determinants of Indian and Chinese behavior and, accordingly, to clarify relationships between actions and perceptions during the conflict.

ACTION DATA: RANK-ORDER SCALING OF CONFLICT BEHAVIOR

The sensitive nature of the border crisis, the location of most important activity in isolated Himalayan country and the strict control of news dissemination by both governments made a problem of acquiring the necessary behavioral information and of checking its accuracy. Data were compiled from several sources. The *New York Times*, *Times* (London), *Statesman* (New Delhi and Calcutta) and *Peking Review* provided most of the relevant information, and the senior author was permitted to examine the excellent files of Dr. Margaret W. Fisher at the University of California (Berkeley), which contributed additional information and made possible several corrections. [8]

We must emphasize again that our investigations have been limited to the twelve days in October when the Sino-Indian border dispute erupted into outright combat. While it is difficult (some would say impossible) to divorce this phase of the conflict from the events which preceded it, we do assume that the hostilities had a dynamic of their own and can be studied accordingly. [9]

It was decided to include for ranking all available activity by China and India of a military nature or affecting military strength. The criterion is not simply one of conflict or violence; rather it entails all behavior with implications for violence. Thus India's revision of its economic allocation priorities and such other acts as curtailing domestic air services were considered relevant. In addition, we included bids (threats, promises, suggestions, and so forth) as well as commissions (physical acts). [10] This decision was reinforced by the consideration that public statements, diplomatic messages and the like also represent behavior. That they were primarily selected for perceptual data should not be cause for concern since the scaling system used reduces the effects of overlap.

The selected behavioral data were divided into twelve days (the ten principal days of this study and the preceding two). Three judges were then called upon to scale the data for each day in terms of level of violence, a dimension of considerable theoretical significance and clearly the most pertinent to the border crisis (Corson, 1970; Azar, 1971a; Azar et al., 1972). The judges were instructed to consider all bids in terms of their believed "violence value": the implication of each for the alleviation, maintenance or aggravation of hostilities. In order to remove the ambiguity occasioned by the conflicting charges of responsibility for the conflict, China was said to have initiated the fighting and to have carried the attack to India. [11]

Because existing scales of international conflict tend to focus on actions short of armed hostilities (Moses et al., 1967; Corson, 1970; Azar, 1971a, 1972), we were obliged to organize our action data in rather new ways reflecting the existence of open combat. Two separate scales were devised for the analysis of Chinese and Indian actions, the first for October 20 and 21, and the second covering October 22 to 31. The idea of the first scale is to provide an opening level of violence for each country for October 22, the day on which coded perceptual data are initially available. The judges were asked to rank Indian and Chinese actions along the following scale for both preliminary days:

Opening Level of Violence Scale (October 21-22, 1962)

0: No violence

1: Public rallies, conferences, meetings with foreign representatives

2: Speeches, diplomatic messages having violence value

3: Supply and defensive operations, mobilizations, requests for aid or use of territory

4: Limited offensive operations (probes, minor infractions of boundaries)

5: Offensive operations in limited territory with limited manpower and weapons

6: Offensive operations at a higher level: greater weapons, more manpower, opening new fronts

A new Violence Increase-Decrease Scale was thus introduced which became the basis for all further evaluations. It makes possible a rank-ordering of days for correlation with perceptual data (Kadane, 1964). As a scaling technique the Increase-Decrease Scale has the virtue of affording continuity over time, something which is sacrificed when each day is considered in isolation. The judges were instructed to consider each day's level of violence from October 22 to 31 the same as the level for the preceding day unless the data specifically suggested otherwise. In this way, changes in the level of violence were always related to each other and the cumulative effects of Chinese attacks and Indian defense efforts maintained despite occasionally weak information. The disparities in available data were also offset by instructions to give value not to each piece of information but only to the total impression for a day. As a result, an abundance of secondary information did not detract from the more significant events, thereby preserving the emphasis on primarily violent behavior.[12]

Violence Increase-Decrease Scale (October 22-31, 1962)

+3: Major increase in violence

+2: Considerable increase in violence

+1: Some increase in violence

0: Continuation of previous day's level

–1: Minor tapering off of previous level

−2: Clearly less violence (withdrawals, acts of conciliation)
−3: Major moves to lessen tensions, remove hostilities

The Chinese and Indian scores, based on averaged rankings of the three judges using both scales, are presented in Table II-1; these figures are depicted graphically in Figure II-2.

THE RELATIONSHIP BETWEEN PERCEPTION AND ACTION

To recapitulate briefly, the objective of this paper is to isolate the determinants of behavior when two states are in armed conflict. Each country's perceptions of itself and its opponent have been inferred from official statements by means of the General Inquirer system of content analysis, and action data have been collected and scaled in terms of levels of violence. It is now possible to analyze the relationship between the two types of data for both states, using the S–r : s–R framework. We have hypothesized that in a conflict situation characterized by armed hostilities one state's actions will be the best predictor of the other's response. That is to say, perceptions are not likely to provide any added information regarding action or events.

Turning first to the question of the relationship between perceptions and behavior, it is clear from the figures in Appendix D that neither

TABLE II-1
ACTION DATA FOR INDIA AND CHINA: LEVEL OF VIOLENCE[a]

Date	China	India
October		
20	5	3
21	6	3
22	8	4
23	9	4.5
24	12	5
25	11	6
26	11.5	7.5
27	12.5	8.5
28	13.5	9
29	13.5	11
30	12.5	12
31	11.5	13

Range = Low (3) to High (13.5)

a. The scores for China and India are **not** related except for those of October 20 and 21. From October 22 to 31 the scores of each scale are internally related only because of the Increase-Decrease Scale.

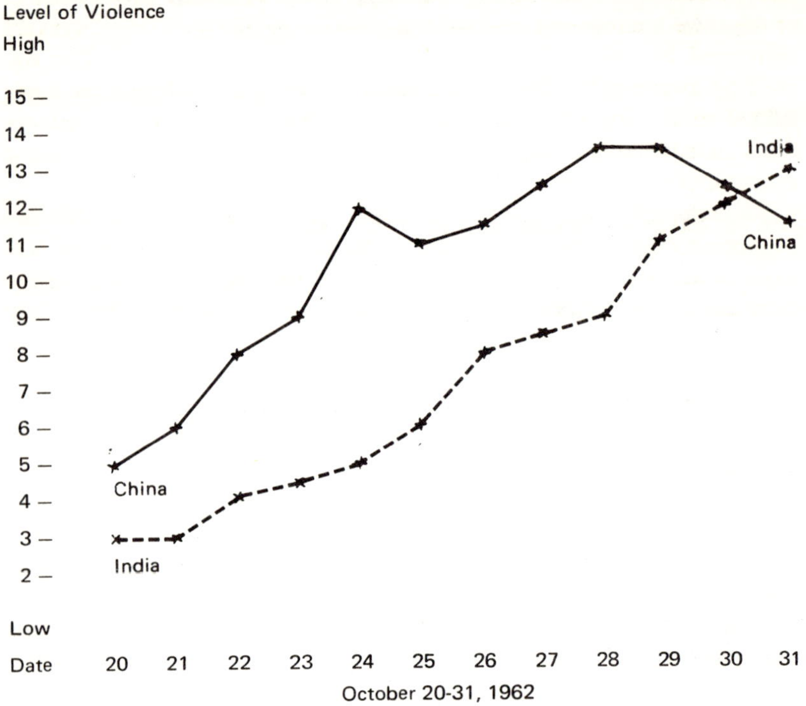

a. See note a, Table II-1.

Figure II-2: INDIAN AND CHINESE VIOLENCE BEHAVIOR[a]

perceptions of the other state nor statements of one's own intent correlate significantly with actions. The sole exception is a perfect correlation between China's perceptions of its own strength and Chinese behavior. However, there are only four days for which Chinese documents were processed, and the identical rank-ordering with behavior is probably artificial.

Two correlation approaches were used in relating (r) and (s) with (R), given an understandabe uncertainty as to the timing of the actual responses we are trying to account for.[13] First, the two variables being studied were drawn from the same day on the assumption that the translation from attitude to action might be immediate. Thus, China's perceptions of Indian negative affect for October 24 were related to its own behavioral response that day. When this approach produced rather weak associations, we decided to allow for the possibility of delayed effects. Because the execution of decisions may be spaced over a number of days, we attempted a selected-aggregate model in which action data are aggregated by selecting day n plus all subsequent days as well. This was done by averaging the relevant day rankings, with the resulting score being related to the perceptual data for day n. Unfortunately, in this instance the selected-aggregate approach failed to improve the correlations because its rankings were identical to those for the same-day model.

In contrast to the weakness of the correlations between perceptions and behavior during the ten days of the border crisis, the findings relating each nation's actions to those of the other are, with one exception, highly significant (see Table II-2). Our hypothesis is at least tentatively confirmed: action, it seems, led quite directly to reaction. The intensity of the conflict was such that both sides were above the level of commitment at which their perceptions, day by day, could be meaningful determinants of their behavior. The situation was sufficiently unambiguous that responses did not have to depend on interpretation: the facts spoke loud enough for themselves. China may have acted according to plan and once attacked India could only respond in kind.

In correlating one state's action with the other's response, two other approaches were used in addition to the same-day model. One-day lag correlations were made twice, the first time with (S) on day n and (R) on n+1, and the second (R) on day n and (S) on n–1 (which allows an extra day in the n count). We also attempted a four-day weighted scheme, the assumption of which is that the behavioral (or perceptual) response to a stimulus will be made on the basis of an imperfect memory covering day n and extending back three days with diminishing recall for each day further from day n. The (S) is accordingly weighted by 4, n–1 by 3, n–2 by 2 and n–3 by 1 (see Zinnes, 1968). The results are then averaged, and this score is related to the (R) or (r and s) for day n. These manipulations improve the correlations, but only marginally.

TABLE II-2
ACTION (S) AND RESPONSE (R)

Models: n =	Same-Day 10	One-Day Lag 9	One-Day Lag 10	Four-Day Weighted 10
China S ↓	r = .676	r = .875	r = .909	r = .915
India R	.05 > P > .01	P < .01	P < .01	P < .01
India S ↓	r = .676	r = .479	r = .676	r = .676
China R	.05 > P > .01	P = n.s.	.05 > P > .01	.05 > P > .01

In sum, the findings reported thus far indicate that the perceptual components of the S–r : s–R model do *not* correlate significantly with its behavioral aspects. Furthermore, none of the perceptual dimensions—affect, potency, activity—is a significant indicator of either state's behavior, with the exception of China's image of itself as strong. The mediating influence of perceptual variables would appear to be minimal in such a high conflict situation. By contrast, each state's actions are highly correlated with the other's actions, as originally hypothesized.

PREDICTING BEHAVIOR[14]

Of course, correlation is not causation, as correlation indicates only the strength of a relationship, not its nature. Having established a strong correlation between Chinese and Indian actions and the relative weakness of correlations between perceptions and behavior, we think it pertinent to examine these relationships once again in a causal framework. This follows from the fact that the interpretation of statistical analyses of time-series data is fraught with pitfalls. A basic reason for the high correlation between two states' actions is that a significant time trend exists in the action data which is not present in perceptual data. Military actions are dependent upon previous actions to a much greater extent than are speeches or messages. That such dependence can produce statistical artifacts is reflected in the coding of the behavioral data since each action was judged in comparison with the previous day's level.[15]

By way of compensation, it is profitable to analyze the relationship between perceptions and the change in action levels, as well as the levels themselves. This is a common statistical device for removing auto-correlation effects and one which we find to have an important bearing on our results.[16] In order to isolate the determinants of behavior we undertook a series of multiple regression analyses so as to predict both levels of violence and changes in violence from day to day. This effort entailed a slight but meaningful modification of the S–r : s–R model. Other studies have found that perceptions do play a significant role in explaining behavior, but only after the effect of action variables has been removed (Milstein and Mitchell, 1968; Milstein, 1968). It makes sense, therefore, to revise the model to allow explicitly for direct linkage between one state's action and another's response, while providing for possible independent effects by perceptions. Reformulated in these terms, the model becomes

```
  r----->s
 ↗        \
 /          \
/            ↘
S---------->R
```

This model was tested by performing multiple regressions (ordinary least squares) with the independent variables being the adversary's behavior and the reacting state's perceptions. As dependent variables we considered the level of violence in R, as before, and then the degree of change in R for both states. In addition, we again allowed for delays in response by lagging the independent variables by one day.

The results presented in Table II-3 indicate that China's actions best predict India's level of violence, but that India's affective perceptions of China measurably increase the statistical significance of the results, both when the independent variables are lagged and when they are not. Perceptions, then, do come into play. Moreover, changes in Indian behavior are best predicted by India's perceptions of itself and China along

TABLE II-3
PREDICTING INDIAN BEHAVIOR

Dependent Variable: Indian Behavior	Independent Variables	Beta	F of Variable	R^2	F of Regression	Level of Significance
Same-Day						
1. t_n	China's behavior: t_n	.71	4.95	.50	4.95	.08
2. t_n	China's behavior: t_n	.84	13.48			
	India-China: positive	–.57	6.15	.80	8.09	.04
One-Day Lag						
3. t_{n+1}	China's behavior: t_n	.76	6.84	.58	6.84	.05
4. t_{n+1}	China's behavior: t_n	.88	14.06			
	India-China: positive	–.58	4.22	.79	7.74	.04
Change in Action Level						
5. $t_n - t_{n-1}$	India-China: weak	–.81	6.32			
	India-India: positive	–1.00	7.91			
	India-China: positive	–.62	3.88	.80	4.02	.15
6. $t_{n+1} - t_n$	India-China: active	1.34	85.58			
	India-India: strong	–.71	23.47			
	India-China: passive	–.20	3.92	.97	34.40	.008

all three dimensions. These results are most significant when the dependent variables are led ($t_{n+1} - t_n$). In other words, when the effects of China's actions are accounted for, India's perceptions of China do contribute to India's level of violence. But changes in Indian violence are predicted best by India's perceptions and not by China's behavior. In fact, when the dependent variable is change in India's action level, other forms of action data—both levels and changes—are never as significant as perceptual data. When independent variables are entered sequentially, perceptual variables appear exclusively until the degrees of freedom are exhausted. [17]

The relevance of perceptions is also evident in the determinants of Chinese behavior. The best predictor of China's level of violence is not India's actions but China's perceptions of its own strength (see Table II-4). This finding is essentially a repetition of the one discussed above. When the independent variables are lagged, Indian actions and perceptions of India as passive emerge as significant. Unfortunately, the predictors of change in China's level of violence cannot be isolated given the low n, and the results yielded are not statistically significant.

These findings are interesting in two respects. First, they offer empirical

TABLE II-4
PREDICTING CHINESE BEHAVIOR

Dependent Variable: Chinese Behavior	Independent Variables	Beta	F of Variable	R^2	F of Regression	Level of Significance
Same-Day						
1. t_n	India's behavior: t_n	.71	4.95	.50	4.95	.08
2. t_n	China-China: strong	.99	7324.00	.99	7324.00	.00015
One-Day Lag						
3. t_{n+1}	India's behavior: t_n	.97	35.29	.946	35.29	.02
4. t_{n+1}	India's behavior: t_n	1.01	1596.03			
	China-India: passive	.23	84.92	.99	800.00	.025
Change in Action Level						
5. $t_n - t_{n-1}$	China-India: passive	1.35	113.40			
	China-China: active	−1.07	71.65	.99	58.01	.09
6. $t_{n+1} -$	China-China: passive	−.81	3.90	.66	3.90	.18

validity to the modified version of the model when examining levels of violence. Behaviors and perceptions have a combined impact which is lost in separate correlations. The revised model portrays this nicely. On the other hand, changes in violence are best explained by the original mediation model, since—and here we are generalizing largely from the Indian case—behaviors seem totally overwhelmed by perceptions. Because the S-R link is so weak in this context, the mediated model is more appropriate. This is ironic when one considers that the S–r : s–R model has seen much more use in analyses for which it is possibly less descriptive or even misleading, as in the case of our own earlier analysis.

Moreover, the findings warrant some reappraisal of the hypothesis presented in this paper. The importance of objective stimuli in the border conflict is evident, but so is the contribution of perceptions. Our initial analysis of correlations seems to have camouflaged as much as it revealed in this regard. By the same token, the importance of S appears to depend on the form of response (R) being studied. It is considerable when the focus is on absolute levels, but it virtually vanishes when changes in behavior are considered.

To summarize, we think our hypothesis is valid as far as it goes, but, alas, it does not go far enough. Although events clearly have predictive power, perceptions continue to influence behavior when states are in armed conflict. This is seen most dramatically when incremental changes in action are the dependent variable, but it is evident also in the case of absolute levels. What was perhaps an overstress on perceptions in other studies induced us to overstress, in turn, the objective facts with which decision makers have to deal. We seem to have ended up somewhere in the middle, acknowledging—with systematic analysis to lean on—the significance of both actual and interpreted definitions of reality.

CONCLUSION

Having gone through elaborate methodological gyrations to reach this point, it might seem bizarre—if not outright cruel—to call into question much of what has been done. Yet this paper is a good example of a study which originated in blissful innocence and ends plagued with serious doubts. The strengths of the enterprise may be summarized briefly: a hypothesis derived from previous work tested and found to be only partially satisfactory, meticulous coding of perceptual and behavioral data, the creation of simple but useful scales to measure levels of violence, and reasonably sophisticated analysis of the data generated. Perhaps these qualities are enough to constitute an exploratory study of modest merit and to provide a meaningful contribution to the literature. Some skepticism is in order, however.

There are several problematic points that need not detain us here: the fact that ten to twelve days were studied in relative isolation of what preceded and followed them; that reliable information was hard to come by, both because the critical events took place in a remote area and because the Chinese are not accustomed to reporting "news"; and that too few documents for perceptual analysis were available to fill even the brief period covered, while the inevitably low n hindered reliable statistical testing. Without meaning to dismiss these limitations facilely, we feel they are less critical than two others more central to the research design.

First, our treatment of perceptions suffers from both an exclusive reliance on official statements and operational rigidity. These are familiar drawbacks to practitioners of automated content analysis. Though familiar, they are serious and a substantial amount of good work is compromised as a consequence. Public documents are selected for coding because they are available, a rare treat in the international field. Unfortunately, these documents serve poorly in portraying how decision makers size up the situations they are confronted with. By virtue of being public or diplomatic, they are designed more to produce an effect than to reveal the mind. There is no known way of detecting camouflage or propaganda in precision-oriented content analysis. A lot of chaff is unavoidably consumed with the wheat and the distortion can be considerable, as we suspect is the case for the Chinese perceptions reported here.[18] Because human judgment is essentially eliminated in the coding process and because every substantive word in a text is given equal weight—regardless of what or where it is—there seems to be no way of coping with this problem. It is not uncommon for an intelligent reading of a document to convey a much different picture from that provided by automated content analysis. The latter is hardly subtle, and the question remains: which is really better? Precision, in any case, is not the same as accuracy, especially when the materials are possibly biased to begin with.[19]

The second limitation worth mentioning concerns the stimulus-response model in whatever form it is used. Earlier we noted our inability to specify the exact response we were trying to account for. An even more troublesome problem is how to identify the true stimulus. In this paper we have assumed an incremental model of decision-making in that our analysis refers to each state's reacting to the other on every day of the conflict, provisions for delayed impact notwithstanding. But an equally if not more persuasive case might be made for the proposition that China's attack was premeditated—meaning that China was not reacting to India's level of violence on October 19 or 20, 1962, or at any time subsequently—and that, once attacked, India had little choice but to galvanize itself (somewhat frantically) both for its immediate defense and long-range security. Under the circumstances, the only stimulus worth considering is the original attack and not what China did thereafter.

If these assessments are accepted, then the strong relationship between S and R is nothing more than an artifact of mutual escalation during the brief period studied. The problem of specifying stimuli is hardly unique to this study, of course. In fact, the border conflict recommended itself to us precisely because it was clear that China and India were preoccupied with each other. In less-confined instances, particularly when events are ambiguous, the problem is increased. Here too the systematic scholar may find himself wondering if he is sacrificing reality for precision.[20]

When all is said and done, this analysis may have shed only limited light on the Sino-Indian border dispute and on international conflict generally. However, we believe that what we have attempted here is part of an ongoing process of trial and error, experimentation and growth in our discipline; we would like to believe that it has made at least a small contribution to theory-building and methodological innovation. Viewed charitably in this context, our investigation represents a halting step, another building block, in the development of new, promising approaches to the study of international politics.

NOTES

1. Our analysis begins with the outbreak of the border war but ends well before the fighting stopped. The period under review was selected primarily for the purpose of examining systematically a tight interaction situation.

2. Lest there be any misunderstanding concerning these remarks, the issue is not whether national leaders respond to a crisis according to their perceptions of it. Of course they do; it could hardly be otherwise. Rather, we are interested in the extent to which perceptions may distort the nature of events (as interpreted by impartial observers not under the same pressure to "do something") so that the responses adopted are ill suited to coping with the problems confronted. In hypothesizing that $S \rightarrow R$ in the Sino-Indian border dispute, we are suggesting that there may be little latitude for perceptual distortion in a conflict of this kind.

3. There are now available several good interpretive studies of the Sino-Indian border dispute and of Sino-Indian relations more broadly defined. Among those which we have found to be informative and thoughtful are, in the order written, Jain (1960); Bains (1962); Sanghvi (1962); Fisher et al. (1963); Van Eekelen (1964); Lamb (1964, 1966); Rowland (1967); Kavic (1967); and most recently Maxwell (1970). See also the Government of India's White Papers (1959-1962) and the official publication on the border conflict from the People's Republic of China (1962). Specific quotes in this section are taken from Reis (1964) or from newspaper sources.

4. Panchshila refers to the "Five Principles of Peaceful Coexistence" contained in a treaty concluded by the Chinese and Indian governments on April 29, 1954, regarding trade relations between India and Tibet. The five principles are mutual respect for each other's territorial integrity and sovereignty, mutual nonaggression, mutual noninterference in each other's internal affairs, equality and mutual benefit and peaceful coexistence.

5. According to Prime Minister Nehru (1962), Peking Radio accused India of attacking Chinese outposts at least an hour before anything had happened.

6. This is one respect in which perceptions were of central importance. If our hypothesis is correct, India's immediate reaction to the movement of Chinese forces against her own was a fairly direct result of that movement. Even if this is so, the Indian leadership still had to assess whether the Chinese attacks were limited in intent or whether they signalled the beginning of a long and costly conflict of major proportions which might spill over into more populated parts of the subcontinent. Whatever its actual judgment, the Indian government gave every impression of accepting the latter scenario, incorrectly as things turned out. (On November 21, a month and one day after the fighting began, the Chinese announced a unilateral cease fire along the entire front and soon thereafter began withdrawing to positions held before the critical events took place.)

7. Only five Chinese documents for the ten days were coded. Twelve Indian documents were coded. See Appendix A for a list of these documents and Appendices B and C for the resulting data on Indian and Chinese perceptions. The different number of documents presents some problems in evaluating the results, but these are not overwhelming since the two sets of documents are analyzed separately and our inferences are drawn accordingly.

8. The scaled action data are not presented in this paper. We would be happy to make them available upon request.

9. See Smoker (1969) for a quantitative analysis of Sino-Indian relations from 1959 to 1964 based on an investigation of communication flows between the Indian and Chinese governments. See also Greaser (1966) and Martin and Young (1966) for related analyses.

10. It has been found that the inclusion of bids as well as commissions in an action scale makes the scale a more satisfactory indicator of subsequent perceptions (Moll, 1964).

11. Attributing the origins of the fighting to China affects only the point of departure in our analysis; it has no repercussion on the investigation as a whole. The same ensuing trends would be discerned even if the reverse assumption were made, holding that India initiated the fighting.

12. The Violence Increase-Decrease Scale can be considered an extension of the Inter-Action Scale developed by Moses et al. (1967) in that it measures behavior which has already erupted into armed conflict.

13. To assess the strength of the relationship between actions and perceptions we used Spearman's Rank Correlation Coefficient (see Siegal, 1956).

14. The nature of the data deviates from standard assumptions underlying the use of conventional statistical and econometric modes of analysis. We are profoundly aware of these limitations. On the other hand, the key issue is not whether assumptions are violated, but how closely the research design approximates the required format. We have sacrificed a measure of statistical propriety for substantive relevance.

15. Recent developments in econometric theory suggest various ways of minimizing distorting effects produced by excessive correlations between variables. Auto-correlation among the observations in the time series provide additional problems in data analysis (see Christ, 1966; Johnston, 1963). These problems are especially salient in the context of this analysis, given an n of twelve days or less. Little is known about small sample properties, but it is generally agreed that conventional statistical and econometric methods run into difficulties when constrained by small samples.

16. A major assumption underlying this corrective procedure is that the auto-correlation parameter (rho) is equal or close to 1. Because of the internal structure of our scales, we have every reason to argue for the near-validity of this assumption.

17. We realize that the progressive loss of degrees of freedom poses serious problems for any analysis of this kind, thereby severely constraining our ability to make inferences. Even so, the statistical results shown in Tables II-3 and II-4 are sufficiently strong that they appear to surmount this problem.

18. On the other hand, the fact that the best predictor of China's level of violence is China's perceptions of its own strength and that other perceptions are also influential may indicate that the Chinese statements are more accurate barometers of subsequent action than we imply here. The question ultimately becomes one of how much confidence one has in the coding schema and other methods employed.

19. The optimum approach, of course, is to combine a judicious reading of the documents with the precision, reliability and replicability of automated content analysis. At present qualitative and quantitative analyses of documentary materials tend to be undertaken separately. The discipline needs to develop ways of combining

both approaches so as to allow for an individual's judgment, sensitivity and expertise as well as the precision and other virtues of quantitative research.

20. Other problems involve the difficulty of distinguishing between an actor's feelings and his intentions. The role of volition is difficult to untangle, thereby adding further ambiguity to (r) and (s) and their interrelationship. See Jervis (1967) for a related critique of the stimulus-response model and the problems of measurement that accompany it. See North (1967) for a response to these criticisms.

REFERENCES

AZAR, E. (1971a) "Analysis of international events." Peace Research Reviews 4 (November).

--- (1971b) "The conflict escalation-reduction cycle: a statistical assessment of interaction shifts." University of North Carolina Studies of Conflict and Peace. (mimeo)

--- (1968) "Scaling data on inter-nation action: a follow-up." Stanford University Studies in International Conflict and Integration. (mimeo)

--- S. COHEN, T. JUKAM, and J. McCORMICK (1972) "Making and measuring the international event as a unit of analysis." University of North Carolina Studies of Conflict and Peace. (mimeo)

BAINS, J. S. (1972) India's International Disputes. Bombay: Asia.

BOULDING, K. C. (1959) "National images and international systems." J. of Conflict Resolution 3 (June): 120-131.

BRODY, R. A. (1966) "Cognition and behavior: a model of inter-state relations," pp. 321-348 in O. J. Harvey (ed.) Experience, Structure and Aaptability. New York: Springer.

China, People's Republic of (1962) The Sino-Indian Boundary Question. Peking: Foreign Language Press.

CHRIST, C. F. (1966) Econometric Models and Methods. New York: John Wiley.

CORSON, W. H. (1970) "Conflict and cooperation in East-West crises: measurement and prediction." Presented at the Events Data Measurement Conference, Michigan State University, East Lansing, Michigan.

DE RIVERA, J. H. (1968) The Psychological Dimension of Foreign Policy. Columbus, Ohio: Charles E. Merrill.

FISHER, M. W., L. E. ROSE, and R. A. HUTTENBACK (1963) Himalayan Battleground: Sino-Indian Rivalry in Ladakh. New York: Frederick A. Praeger.

GREASER, C. (1966) "Sino-Indian border dispute, 1954-1962." M.A. thesis. University of Southern California.

HOLSTI, O. R. (1968) "Content analysis," pp. 596-692 in Volume II of G. Lindzey and E. Aronson (eds.) The Handbook of Social Psychology. Reading, Mass.: Addison-Wesley.

--- (1965) "The 1914 case." Am. Pol. Sci. Rev. 59 (June): 365-378.

--- R. A. BRODY, and R. C. NORTH (1964a) "Theory and measurement of interstate behavior: a research application of automated content analysis." Stanford University Studies in International Conflict and Integration. (unpublished)

--- (1964b) "Measuring affect and action in international reaction models: empirical materials from the 1962 Cuban crisis." J. of Peace Research 1: 170-189.

HOLSTI, O. R., R. C. NORTH, and R. A. BRODY (1968) "Perception and action in the 1914 crisis," pp. 123-158 in J. D. Singer (ed.) Quantitative International Politics: Insights and Evidence. New York: Free Press.

India, Ministry of External Affairs (1959-1962) "Notes, memoranda and letters exchanged between the governments of India and China." White Papers I-VII. New Delhi.

JAIN, G. (1960) Panchsheela and After: Sino-Indian Relations in the Context of the Tibetan Insurrection. Bombay: Asia.

JERVIS, R. (1968) Hypotheses on misperception." World Politics 20 (April): 454-479.

--- (1967) "The cost of the scientific study of politics: an examination of the Stanford content analysis studies." International Studies Q. 11 (December): 366-393.

JOHNSTON, J. (1963) Econometric Methods. New York: McGraw-Hill.

KADANE, J. B. (1964) "Alternative methods of scaling action data." Stanford University Studies in International Conflict and Integration. (mimeo)

KAVIC, L. J. (1967) India's Quest for Security, Defence Policies 1947-1965. Berkeley: Univ. of California Press.

LAMB, A. (1966) The McMahon Line: A Study in the Relations between India, China, and Tibet, 1904 to 1914, Volumes I and II. London: Routledge & Kegan Paul.

--- (1964) The China-India Border, The Origins of the Disputed Boundaries. London: Oxford Univ. Press.

MARTIN, W. R. and R. A. YOUNG (1966) "World event-interaction study: pilot study report." University of Michigan. (mimeo)

MAXWELL, N. (1970) India's China War. London: Jonathan Cape.

McCLELLAND, C. A. and G. D. HOGGARD (1969) "Conflict patterns in interactions among nations," pp. 711-724 in J. N. Rosenau (ed.) International Politics and Foreign Policy: A Reader in Research and Theory. New York: Free Press.

McNEMAR, Q. (1955) Psychological Statistics. New York: John Wiley.

MILSTEIN, J. S. (1968) "The Vietnam war, 1965-1967: an empirical analysis of the dynamics of escalation." Ph.D. dissertation. Stanford University.

--- and W. C. MITCHELL (1969) "Dynamics of the Vietnam conflict: a quantitative analysis and predictive computer simulation," pp. 162-213 in W. Isard (ed.) Vietnam: Issues and Alternatives. Cambridge, Mass.: Schenkman.

MITCHELL, W. C. and C. CUYKENDALL (1971) "What does an integrated data base have to do with British foreign policy from 1970-1914?" presented at the Western Political Science Association Meetings, Albuquerque, New Mexico.

MOLL, K. (1964) "Correlation of perceptions with actions in the Cuban crisis." Stanford University Studies in International Conflict and Integration. (mimeo)

MOSES, L. E., R. A. BRODY, O. R. HOLSTI, J. B. KADANE, and J. S. MILSTEIN (1967) "Scaling data on inter-nation action." Science 156 (May): 1054-1059.

NEHRU, J. (1962) "Address to ministers." October 25.

NORTH, R. C. (1967) "Research pluralism and the international elephant." International Studies Q. 11 (December): 394-416.

--- (1964) "The behavior of nation states." Stanford University Studies in International Conflict and Integration. (mimeo)

--- and O. R. HOLSTI (1963) "Hostility and economic variables." Stanford University Studies in International Conflict and Integration. (mimeo)

NORTH, R. C., R. A. BRODY, and O. R. HOLSTI (1963) "Some empirical data on the conflict spiral." Stanford University Studies in International Conflict and Integration. (mimeo)

OSGOOD, C., G. SUCI, and P. H. TANNENBAUM (1957) The Measurement of Meaning. Urbana: Univ. of Illinois Press.

PRUITT, D. G. (1965) "Definition of the situation as a determinant of international action," pp. 391-432 in H. C. Kelman (ed.) International Behavior: A Social-Psychological Analysis. New York: Holt, Rinehart & Winston.

REIS, F. S. (1964) "Chronology of the Sino-Indian border controversy, 1947-1962." Stanford University (mimeo)

ROWLAND, J. (1967) A History of Sino-Indian Relations, Hostile Co-existence. Princeton, N.J.: Van Nostrand.

SANGHVI, R. (1962) India's Northern Frontier and China. Bombay: Contemporary.

SIEGAL, S. (1956) Nonparametric Statistics for the Behavioral Sciences. New York: McGraw-Hill.

SIVERSON, R. M. (1972) "Role and decision-making in the Suez crisis: the cases of Israel and Egypt." Presented at the Annual Meeting of the Peace Research Society (International)/Western Region, Vancouver, B.C.

SMOKER, P. (1969) "A time series analysis of Sino-Indian relations." J. of Conflict Resolution 13 (June): 172-191.

STONE, P. J. (1966) The General Inquirer: A Computer Approach to Content Analysis. Cambridge, Mass.: M.I.T. Press.

TANTER, R. (1972) "International system and foreign policy approaches: implications for conflict modelling and management," in R. Tanter and R. Ullman (eds.) "Theory and policy in international relations." World Politics, Supplementary Issue.

VAN EEKELEN, W. F. (1964) Indian Foreign Policy and the Border Dispute with China. The Hague: Martinus Nijhoff.

VERBA, S. (1961) "Assumptions of rationality and non-rationality in models of the international system." World Politics 14 (October): 93-117.

ZANINOVITCH, M. G. (1964) "An empirical theory of state response: the Sino-Soviet case." Ph.D. dissertation. Stanford University.

ZINNES, D. A. (1968) "The expression and perception of hostility in prewar crisis: 1914," pp. 85-119 in J. D. Singer (ed.) Quantitative International Politics: Insight and Evidence. New York: Free Press.

--- (1966) "A comparison of hostile behavior of decision-makers in simulate and historical data." World Politics 18 (April): 474-502.

APPENDIX A
LIST OF CODED DOCUMENTS

Chinese Documents (1962):[a]

- October 22: Defense Ministry Statement
- October 24: Chinese Proposals to India
- October 24: Chou En-Lai Letter to Nehru
- October 27: *Renmin Ribao* Editorial
- October 28: Peng-Chen Address

Indian Documents (1962):[b]

- October 22: Prime Minister Nehru Broadcast
- October 23: Indian Memorandum to China
- October 24: Indian Response to China
- October 25: Nehru Address to Ministers
- October 26: Ministry of E. A. Note to China[c]
- October 26: Chakravarty Address to U.N.
- October 26/27: Nehru Letter to Heads of State
- October 27: Nehru Letter to Chou En-Lai
- October 28: Ministry of E. A. Note to China
- October 30: Ministry of E. A. Note to China
- October 31: Ministry of E. A. Note to China
- October 31: Ministry of E. A. Memorandum to China

a. With the exception of the **Renmin Ribao** editorial the Chinese documents are official publications of the People's Republic of China.

b. All Indian documents were officially released by the Government of India.

c. Ministry of E. A. refers to Ministry of External Affairs, Government of India.

APPENDIX B
INDIAN PERCEPTIONS[a]

October	Positive	Negative	Strong	Weak	Active	Passive
India Perceives India						
22	26.2	11.0	29.4	1.0	25.0	7.4
24	34.1	3.7	19.5	8.6	13.1	20.7
25	8.0	2.8	42.6	4.6	32.8	9.2
26	10.0	7.8	27.4	11.2	26.8	16.8
27	23.0	6.3	25.2	6.1	15.4	24.0
28	4.4	17.4	26.1	13.0	30.4	8.7
30	33.3	0.0	33.3	0.0	0.0	33.3
31	22.2	7.5	29.6	0.0	29.6	11.1
Total	161.2	56.5	233.1	44.5	173.4	131.2
Mean	20.2	7.1	29.1	5.6	21.7	16.4
India Perceives China						
22	2.8	25.5	44.3	0.0	27.4	0.0
24	5.0	25.0	40.0	0.0	30.0	0.0
25	6.5	19.6	14.0	0.0	55.4	4.4
26	3.2	20.4	36.2	1.6	35.4	3.2
27	6.0	17.9	38.5	1.7	28.2	7.7
28	6.4	9.7	22.6	16.1	45.2	0.0
30	0.0	42.9	19.0	0.0	38.1	0.0
31	15.6	3.1	46.9	3.1	28.2	3.1
Total	45.5	164.1	261.5	22.5	287.9	18.4
Mean	5.7	20.5	32.7	2.8	36.0	2.3

a. Figures are derived from the formula $\frac{\text{Variable (100)}}{\text{Total}}$

APPENDIX C
CHINESE PERCEPTIONS[a]

October	Positive	Negative	Strong	Weak	Active	Passive
China Perceives China						
22	100.0	0.0	0.0	0.0	0.0	0.0
24	11.6	18.0	28.0	2.7	20.1	19.6
27	9.3	13.2	31.4	10.8	27.0	8.3
28	8.7	17.4	39.1	0.0	13.1	21.7
Total	129.6	48.6	98.5	13.5	60.2	49.6
Mean	32.4	12.1	24.6	3.4	15.1	12.4
China Perceives India						
22	0.0	26.1	45.1	0.0	28.8	0.0
24	5.0	22.6	36.0	1.0	27.3	8.1
27	4.1	23.3	37.4	1.9	29.0	4.3
28	0.0	66.7	33.3	0.0	0.0	0.0
Total	9.1	138.7	151.8	2.9	85.1	12.4
Mean	2.3	34.7	37.9	0.7	21.3	3.1

a. Figures are derived from the formula $\frac{\text{Variable (100)}}{\text{Total}}$

APPENDIX D
CORRELATIONS OF PERCEPTION AND ACTION

D_1: Perceptions of the Other State (r) and Behavioral Response (R)

		Models	
Actor (perceiver)	Perception[a]	Same-Day	Selected-Aggregate
India	China negative	r = –.476 P = n.s.	Same
	China strong	r = –.071 P = n.s.	Same
	China active	r = –.185 P = n.s.	Same
China	India negative	r = .400 P = n.s.	Same
	India strong	r = –.800 P = n.s.	Same
	India active	r = –.400 P = n.s.	Same

a. For reasons of parsimony only the negative, strong and active directions are shown for the three perceptual dimensions. Their opposites are no more revealing.

D_2: Perception of Self (s) and Behavioral Response (R)

		Models	
Actor (perceiver)	Perception[a]	Same-Day	Selected-Aggregate
India	India negative	r = –.095 P = n.s.	Same
	India strong	r = .238 P = n.s.	Same
	India active	r = .107 P = n.s.	Same
China	China negative	r = .400 P = n.s.	Same
	China strong	r = 1.00 P = .05	Same
	China active	r = .400 P = n.s.	Same

a. For reasons of parsimony only the negative, strong and active directions are shown for the three perceptual dimensions. Their opposites are no more revealing.

Chapter III

CRISIS DECISION-MAKING AND COGNITIVE BALANCE

Murray L. Adelman

The study of international politics has traditionally been concerned with actions of nation-states in the international arena (combined with some concern for certain internal characteristics such as size, geographical placement and topography, population, industry, and so on). It has been assumed that one could predict the behavior of a nation through knowledge of the actions of the other states with which it dealt in the international system. The process was considered to be one of a "rational" give and take. While a nation was observing certain rules or norms of the system, it was expected to react to the actions of another on a like basis in accordance with its more or less enlightened self-interest. Even the term employed in diplomacy for the motive force of a state's behavior, *raison d'état,* emphasized its rational, almost mechanistic, character.

THEORIES OF COGNITIVE BALANCE

Diplomatic historians or political analysts could thus explain all behavior by reference to this *raison d'état,* and, in the quest for historical explanation, articulate it even if the nation's leaders had not. This is not to say these students of international affairs did not refer to documents and archives while attempting to plumb the motivation of their subjects. But there was no systematic attempt to utilize these sources, and rarely was an effort made to generalize about leaders' motivations and behavior in typical situations except with reference again to national interest, *raison d'état,* dynastic or imperial aggrandizement, or power.

Such approaches to the study of international politics have now been supplemented with attempts to link international politics to other systematic work in human behavior. General systems theory and information theory have made the international level amenable to scientific study, while an alternative, but complementary, way of handling the problem has been that broadly labeled the decision-making approach. The essence of this approach is that the decision makers (those occupying the formal and informal roles giving one the ability to commit the nation's resources to a course of action) should be the focus of analysis. It is their "definition of the situation" or perceptions of the actions of others, and their definition of policy or plans, which mediate between the stimulus of another nation's act and their own consequent behavior. The emphasis here may be either on organizational variables (Snyder, 1966) or on psychological variables (North, 1968). The development of various content-analytic techniques and the wealth of relevant social-psychological models and theories encourage the latter emphasis.

Social psychology has given to political science a wealth of theoretical schemes which for a number of reasons have seemed particularly appropriate for the decision-making approach. Primarily, social psychologists are concerned with similar sorts of problems—the formation, maintenance, and modification of attitudes, values, and images. One of the most well-known of these schema has been that of cognitive balance (Newcomb, 1959, 1958, 1953; Heider, 1946; Osgood and Tannenbaum, 1955). Much theoretical and empirical work has been done in this field, providing the conceptual basis for some of the newer work in decision-making.

The purpose of this study, then, is to apply a cognitive balance model to the study of international politics, particularly to the problem of crisis decision-making. The statements of key decision makers of the United States and the Soviet Union, as derived from publicly available documents from two separate crisis situations, will be analyzed by a method of theme scaling. The two periods studied are the Bay of Pigs invasion of 1961 and the Cuban missile crisis of 1962.

The basis of this approach is that individuals perceive other actors and related objects, attributes, issues and so forth, in some cognitively balanced manner; i.e., an individual is assumed to experience psychological pressures when he perceives related environmental objects in a cognitively contradictory manner. That is, if actor A is negatively oriented (here employing Theodore Newcomb's terminology) toward a given object (X) at the same time perceiving that actor B positively relates toward that same object, there will be psychological strain toward an equilibrium, one of the states of which may be that actor A will relate negatively toward actor B (Newcomb, 1958).

Conversely, if actor A is positively oriented toward X, and perceives that actor B is also positively oriented toward the same X, then he will be positively oriented toward B. The major proposition is that there is a strain toward symmetry in an actor's phenomenal system. In other words, perceptions of difference with other actors in cognitive orientations toward environmental objects (which might include an attribute of one or both of the actors) leads to negative orientations toward those actors, while perceptions of similarities toward a given X leads to positive evaluations of other actors.

If one thus diagrams the systems discussed above, one finds the set of balanced and imbalanced cognitive structures for a given actor shown in Figure III-1.

One can summarize these relationships thus: A system is balanced when all the relationships have a positive sign, or when two of them are negative and one positive.

There are actually several systems involved in these sets of bonds. The phenomenal system presented above includes only the orientations as they exist for one of the actors, while the social system includes all the orientations of all the actors. of which there are eight:

(1) The orientation ("attraction") of A to B
(2) B's perception of that attraction
(3) B's attraction to A
(4) A's perception of B's attraction
(5) A's orientation ("attitude") to X
(6) B's perception of this attitude
(7) B's attitude to X
(8) A's perception of that attitude

Presumably all relationships are of a balanced nature in the long run, that is, all tend toward equilibrium or a homeostatic condition which involves the absence of psychological strain or tension. The problem that arises here is one of the dynamics of dealing with imbalance. Newcomb (1958: 250), positing his scheme as a model of "communicative acts," attempts to treat the problem of imbalance by stating as a first premise that following a communication from A to B about perceived discrepancies in their attitudes toward X, the chances are that A and B's

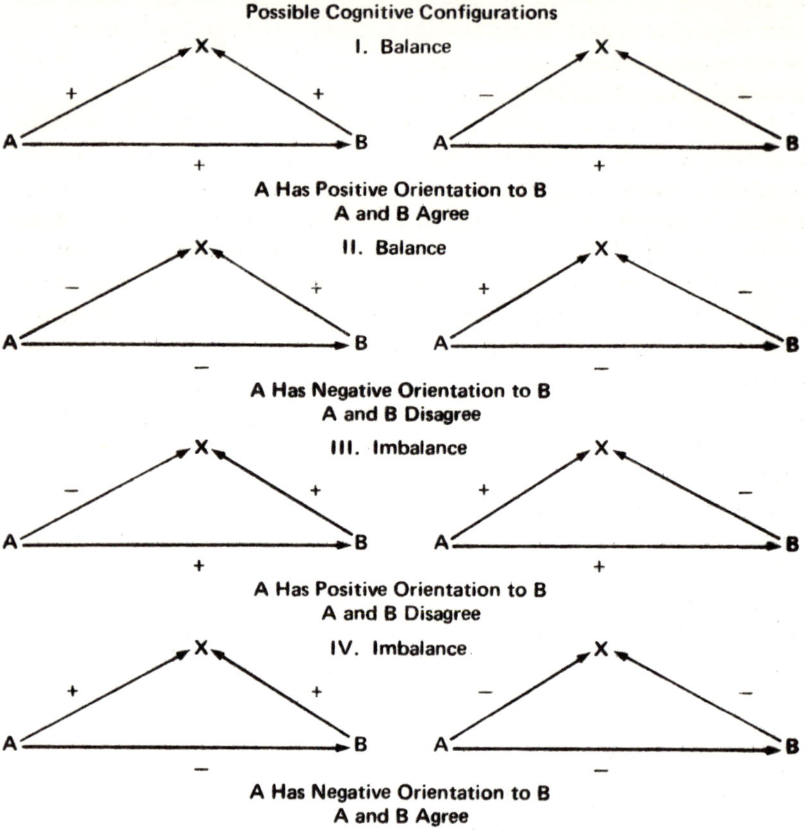

SOURCE: Taylor (1968).

Figure III-1: CONFIGURATIONS OF BALANCE AND IMBALANCE

orientation to X will become more similar than before. However, this proposition holds true only if the recipient of the communication trusts the transmitters or, more formally stated: "The probabilities of increased similarity following a communication vary with the degree of positive attraction on the part of the receiver toward the transmitter."

There is also a converse aspect to this general proposition. A communication is more likely to occur between persons if their orientations to the object differ in some respect than if they do not differ. This occurs hypothetically if the two actors are part of the same group. This does not seem to be the case in international politics when the actors are decision makers of rival or hostile nations involved in a crisis situation.

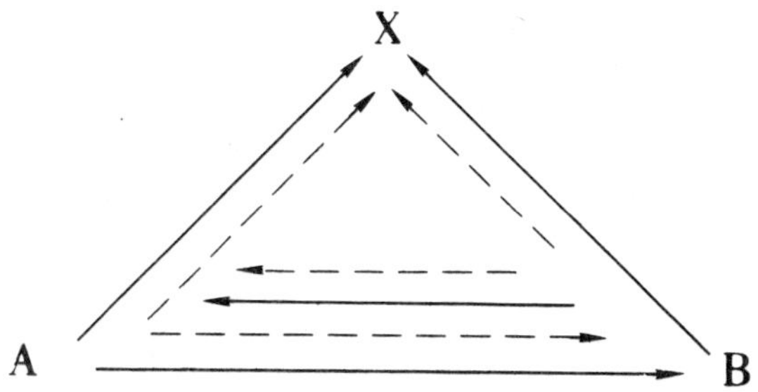

SOURCE: Newcomb (1958).

Figure III-2: THE SOCIAL SYSTEM OF AN A-B-X BOND

When an imbalance for foreign policy decision makers has reached such a stage, the actors have presumably attempted to co-orient each other and have failed. Thus international communication should decrease in such a situation. As Holsti (1965) has shown in his study of the 1914 crisis, the proportion of intercoalition (as contrasted with intracoalition) communication decreases because, although such communication becomes more urgent, it simultaneously becomes more difficult.

This finding is congruent with Newcomb's theory that the similarity-producing effects of communication vary with the attraction among the communicators. Thus, if two or more potential communicators are indifferent to one another, or mistrust each other's motives, the mere fact of discrepancy in orientations toward X would not necessarily lead to communication. The probabilities of communication concerning an X, therefore, will vary jointly with the discrepancy in orientation of the potential communicators and with the strength of the positive attraction among them. However, as Festinger et al. (1950) report, if the actors have strong motivation for keeping the social system functioning as such, an increase in the amount of communication between those actors who are hostile is likely.

The emphasis in this discussion has been on orientations of other actors as perceived by an individual as well as on actual attitudes, because it is the perceptions of these orientations upon which the actors base their decisions for communication and on which they base their attraction for the other actor. But we do know that judgments about discrepancies are often not accurate, and that distortion of one's perception for a variety of reasons occurs with great frequency in political situations despite the assumption of full information and "rationality" upon which diplomatic historians, among others, base their work. When rigorous techniques are applied to international decision-making phenomena we find that distortion, particularly in a crisis situation, does take place.

Distortion is one of many ways of handling imbalance and, in terms of any content analysis technique now being used, the only one that can be easily measured. Distortion effects will be further discussed below, as will other psychological devices for dealing with cognitive imbalance and reduction of strain.

(1) A change in an actor's orientation in the direction of the other's as perceived: if the actor felt a low commitment to the object, and the relationship between A and B were of great salience, this could result. On the other hand, if the object were of central value, resistance to change would be high.

(2) Perception of change in the other's orientation in one's own direction: the probabilities of this occurring will vary with the degree of accuracy of one's perception of the other's orientation. Thus, if A's existing strain has, as hypothesized, led to one or more communications from him to B, and if these communications have had the effect of making B's orientations more like A's, then relatively accurate perceptions of change in B's orientations are more likely to occur. Conversely, relatively inaccurate or distorted perceptions of change in B's orientation are more likely to take place under opposite conditions—an absence of further opportunity for exchange of information with B (which is what occurs under conditions of crisis stress).

Distortion, then, is most likely to occur when there is no further opportunity for either persuasion or reality-testing by means of communication, when strain toward similarity is highest, and when other alternatives are least welcome. For example, A may be able to convince himself that a perceived discrepancy with B in regard to X (to which A is highly committed), in the absence of any communication on the subject with B, was all a mistake or at least greatly exaggerated. Distortion of perception can also occur under exactly opposite conditions, that is, when discovery of discrepancy leads to reduction of attraction to B. Under such circumstances, there may be a tendency to distort the amount of discrepancy because reduction of attraction would presumably have led to reduced overall communication between the co-communicators. This leads to a consideration of the third alternative.

(3) Reduced attraction toward the other actor: the choice of this alternative can be either general or specific in nature; i.e., there may be

either a decrease in one's overall attraction to the other actor, or a decline in attraction which is specific only to that particular X (more of this below). The conditions leading one to choose this third alternative are: (a) when commitment to one's existing orientation is high, (b) conditions making for distorted perception of the other's orientation are not present, (c) persuading the other to one's own orientation is ruled out and (d) relevance is so high that one cannot readily leave the field. One or any combination of these would lead to a greater likelihood of reduced attraction to the other actor.

(4) Reduced valence toward the object of communication seen as a compromise solution to the problem of strain: thus, if all other alternatives are too costly, one can, without changing the nature of one's own orientation, convince oneself that the matter is basically unimportant. This alternative might be chosen under those circumstances where the maintenance of positive A-B attraction is important to the actor, and where other common Xs are seen as more relevant. However, if the same person is involved in many overlapping A-B-X systems, and if the same X is involved in many of these (with different Bs) and if the valence toward the common X is strong in all or most of the other systems, the alternative of reducing valence is not likely to be chosen. An example of the reduction of the valence of X, particularly where A finds it desirable to maintain a positive attraction to B, is the phrase signifying détente, "let bygones be bygones." In other words, the old divisive issues are no longer so important, and other Xs (toward which their attitudes are similar) have supplanted them in saliency.

This scheme implies certain basic assumptions. First, before strain or imbalance can be induced, the perceived discrepancies must be with actors who, for some reason, are important in a given situation. There may be actors to whom one is so indifferent that perceived discrepancies with them would not induce any amount of strain. However, this is not likely to be the case when one is studying the perceptions of two actors involved in an international crisis situation.

Second, the object or value which is negatively or positively cathected must also be important to one of the actors. As Rosenberg et al. (1960: 17-18) point out, a tendency to respond to given Xs with either positive or negative affect

> is accompanied by a cognitive structure made up of beliefs about the potentialities of that object for attaining or blocking the realization of valued states. . . . thus strong and stable positive affect toward a

> given object should be associated with beliefs about the potentialities of that object for attaining or blocking the realization of valued states: the sign (positive or negative) and extremity of the affect felt toward the object are correlated with the content of its associated cognitive structure.

If, for example, A's affective orientation toward the X approaches indifference, then perceived nonconsensus with B in relation to X will produce little strain. The objects which decision makers tend to discuss in public statements (those that researchers usually treat as their data) are typically those involving the attainment of goals, and are therefore cognitively salient.

Third, the object must have joint relevance to both actors. If A perceives no common impact upon both himself and B from X, there is little reason to believe that strain will follow from A's perception of discrepancy. Again it is reasonable to assume that objects discussed by decision makers, particularly during periods of crisis, do have joint relevance, otherwise there would be little point in devoting attention (always a scarce resource for decision makers) to their mention or elucidation.

A major criticism of the various cognitive balance or dissonance theories is that, since so many different strategies of strain or dissonance reduction are proposed, it is difficult, if not impossible, to falsify a hypothesis derived from these schemes. All outcomes appear to support the theories. But, as Holsti (1967) indicates, and as discussed above, if the specific conditions are present the hypothesized outcome can be falsified.

MULTIDIMENSIONALITY

Most of the balance theories are elaborated as if the attraction toward A and B were a unitary or unidimensional relationship. Newcomb (1958: 250) mentions that although positive and negative attraction are often generalized, for most cases this attraction does have limits and is more or less specific to the X in question. However, most research has not focused on the question of whether or not these orientations are in fact multi- or unidimensional. Rosenberg et al. (1960: 160) mention "cognitive files," implying that for any given other actor, an actor has a repertoire of Xs with which that other is associated. If this is true, then one can speak of conditions under which an actor's cognitive files expand or contract, or in Scott's (1966: 70) terms, the "dimensional complexity" of one's image of another nation can vary over time and between individuals. He states, "An attribute structure is complex to the extent that it comprises a large number of independent dimensions for describing objects."

The existence of multidimensionality or the issue-specificity of actor orientations is indicated in the works of political scientists not directly involved in the study of international politics. Dahl (1961) has shown that the leadership in the political system is determined by the nature of the particular conflict, and that participation in a coalition involved in making decisions varies according to the issue area. Alker (1964) and Russett (1966), in their studies of the dimensions of conflict in General Assembly voting, have shown that coalitions are composed differently depending on the kind of issue in dispute. Thus, if coalitions at different social levels (participation in which would imply a certain degree of positive attraction) are differently composed at different times, one is led to conclude that an actor's orientation toward another is neither positive, negative, nor even neutral, per se, but is a complex of "suborientations," any of which may be differently placed on an evaluational continuum depending on the particular significant environmental stimulus at issue.

Thus, if one is interested in studying crisis and the interaction between the impact of the international system and of the perceptions and consequent actions of decision makers, the question arises as to the mutual effects of international crisis and cognitive complexity. Rosenberg et al. (1960: 161) hypothesize that "appropriate 'cognitive material' though 'filed' may be unavailable because of the functional stupidity and cognitive rigidity that seem to occur under conditions of high anxiety that occur when a person is in intense conflict."

In other words, in a crisis situation an actor tends to simplify his image of the enemy, to block out favorable or positive suborientations toward the other, and to distort or block out positive information which would modify the highly negative orientation produced by the X or Xs evoking the crisis.

Various kinds of stress, frustration and threat situations do appear to produce a change toward cognitive simplicity. Sherif with Sherif (1967: 348) report results showing that along with a heightening of contrast effect (discussed below) increased ego-involvement brings about a reduction in the number of categories used by highly involved subjects in comparison to less committed individuals in sorting statements relevant to their own attitude. Shroeder et al. (1967: 98 ff.) report that under conditions of "superoptimal noxity," the information processing and decision-making capabilities decrease. However, the interesting observation is that some noxity does increase perceptual and decision-making abstractness to a point, but that these abilities quickly decline after that optimum has been reached.

This finding is important for our purposes; it raises the question of whether the international crises one selects for study are of sub- or superoptimal noxity. In the absence of systematic ways of comparing crises for noxity, it is very difficult to predict whether the variables which have been here discussed will actually operate in the manner specified. It is also entirely possible that some crises, though seen as extremely important in affecting the international system, may not have actually produced such stress for the participants as to bring about the psychological states we have been describing. This shall be discussed later.

Certain findings by those employing the Inter-Nation Simulation are particularly enlightening with regard to cognitive complexity. Driver (1965: D-79) in analyzing the perceptions of his surrogates in the simulated situation found that the stress of threat

> reduced the complexity of the decision-makers' perceptions, thus eliminating an awareness of the military power of other nations, i.e., causing loss of awareness of deterrents. . . . Threat was strongly related to perceptual simplicity, which in turn is related strongly to war. A lack of awareness of the deterrents appears related to reduction in perceptual complexity.

The relation is a complex one in that the direction of causality is not well specified in this work. Driver (1965: D-79-80) states the findings again in a slightly different manner:

> An examination of factors related to aggression vs. non-aggression for 32 large powers revealed that the possession of complex cognitive structures by the decision-makers is associated with infrequent occurrences of aggressive behaviors; and contrariwise, less complex cognitive structures seem closely linked with the expression of much aggressive behavior. In other words, only complex nations are likely to be non-aggressive, but under certain circumstances they can become aggressive; while nations with simple structures are almost always aggressive.

The question implied here is a crucial one: Does cognitive simplicity bring about aggressive behavior in threatening situations, or does threat or intense conflict bring about cognitive simplicity? Driver is a bit ambiguous, but the weight of his evidence seems to indicate the latter situation, which corroborates Holsti (1963) and Rosenberg et al. (1960). Pruitt (1966: 396) cites evidence from various studies also showing that "People tend to become rigid and repetitive under stress. They think up fewer new alternatives and are, therefore, more likely to persist in old, maladaptive approaches."

PERCEPTUAL DISTORTION

It has been a basic axiom in social psychology that all perception is selective, forced on one by the nature of the cognitive apparatus. What differentiates human perception in times of crisis from that of noncrisis is that the pressures of time, the very necessity to act, compels decision makers to cut short the resources of time, energy and attention which they might ordinarily give a problem. Given sufficient time, it is argued, the decision maker could perhaps thoroughly survey all possible alternatives to action, all possible interpretations of intentions of the opponent, and the consequences of his own policies in selecting one interpretation over another; or he might be able to check and recheck numerous facts concerning the capabilities of the opponent in relation to his own military and political resources. But as Bruner (1958: 87) points out,

> a constant regimen of close inspection of events, a devotion to the alternative ways in which events may be perceived, may conflict with requirements for action. We are forced to decide whether a man is honest or not, whether a group is friendly toward us. . . . We cannot, like Hamlet, remain long in the state of being "sicklied o'er with the pale cast of thought"—not if we are to act.

An experiment with word recognition by Bruner (1958: 91) suggests that the inaccuracy of perception is likely to increase when greater speed is required, as one might expect under stress conditions of a crisis. This phenomenon occurs because

> To gain speed, we limit the alternative hypotheses that we are willing to entertain. In the event of ambiguous stimulation, as in social perception generally and in international crisis decision-making in particular, such speed-producing monopolistic hypotheses are likely to be confirmed. We expect, for example, a hostile action from a disliked person; he does something equivocal; we "see" it as a hostile act and thus confirm our expectation. It is the case, moreover, that under conditions where alternative expectancies must be limited we will be more likely to adopt social conventional expectancies or ones that reflect our more basic needs. It is in this sense that stress and social pressure serve to reduce the subtlety of the registration process.

The definition of distortion that will be employed in this study is one closely related to that of Sherif. The concepts of assimilation and contrast effects have been developed by Sherif et al. (1965: 18 ff.; see also Sherif, 1967; Sherif with Sherif, 1967, Sherif and Hovland, 1961) to explain changes in one's latitude of

(1) acceptance, defined as the area on an issue continuum which is "the most acceptable position plus other positions the individual also finds acceptable";
(2) rejection, defined as "the most objectionable to the individual, the thing most detested in a particular domain, plus other items or positions also objectionable to him";
(3) noncommitment, defined as "the positions he does not evaluate as either acceptable or objectionable." Included in this category are the "don't know," "neutral," "undecided," "no opinion" or "no comment" replies to public opinion surveys.

According to Sherif et al. (1965), the range of acceptance is thus viewed as including (aside from that expressing most closely one's own attitude) the positions with which one will agree, even if they are somewhat discrepant from one's own. Assimilation is thus the process of shifting or bringing views which are discrepant into one's latitude of acceptance. A reverse process occurs in the formation of one's latitude of rejection. Those views which are discrepant from one's own, but which one cannot agree with or find acceptable, are thrust out of the area of acceptance, and shifted or placed into the area of rejection (provided, of course, that the position in question does not fall into the area of noncommitment), and contrasted to one's own, that is, perceived as far from one's own attitude. In other words, attitudes which are "objectively" distant may be assimilated under certain conditions, while under opposite conditions positions which are objectively close may be viewed as quite distant and pushed into the latitude of rejection, which itself may be displaced to a far distance.

The dynamic which regulates the size of the latitudes of acceptance and rejection and determines the degree of assimilation and contrast is the degree of ego-involvement in the issue area. The degree of ego-involvement in the Sherif et al. studies is defined as the extremity of one's own position on the attitude dimension. Sherif with Sherif (1967: 348) states that "there is considerable evidence from other research showing a general relationship between extremity of position and degree of involvement in an issue."

Osgood and Tannenbaum (1955: 46) report similar findings in their studies of congruity in attitude change. They state that

> in terms of producing attitude change, the total pressure toward congruity is distributed between the objects of judgment associated by an assertion in inverse proportion to their separate degrees of polarization. In other words, relatively less polarized objects of judgment, when associated with relatively more polarized objects of

judgment, absorb proportionately greater amounts of pressure toward congruity, and consequently change more.

Thus, when ego-involvement is high, the latitude of acceptance decreases, while the latitude of rejection increases ("as a curvilinear function of the extremity of the person's commitment"). At the same time the latitude of noncommitment also decreases in a curvilinear manner, approaching zero for subjects with the greatest ego-involvement. Sherif and Sherif (1967: 348) report that a zero latitude of noncommitment occurs with "an appreciable number of highly committed subjects." They find that a subject's placement of discrepant communications will manifest a "raised threshold for acceptance and a lowered threshold for rejection . . . to the extent that he is ego-involved, wittingly or unwittingly." When a subject is committed, then, his latitude of rejection becomes "disproportionately greater" than his latitude of acceptance. Thus, the greater one's ego-involvement, the greater is the tendency for one's judgments (in terms of placements of communications on a continuum) to form a more bimodal distribution with one side (corresponding to the latitude of rejection) and the middle (the latitude of noncommitment) considerably shrunken. As ego-involvement or relevance of an issue area increases, there is a tendency for an individual to polarize various positions on an attitudinal continuum, with a great amount of displacement occurring in the process of assimilating or contrasting discrepant views, depending on the extent of the discrepancy from one's own position (the anchor, in Sherif et al.'s terminology).[1]

Although the discussion of assimilation-contrast effects does not directly deal with international crisis, we can see how it integrates with much crisis literature. Ego-involvement, or extremity of attitude or orientation is a concomitant of crisis, and thus should increase when such situations occur. We should thus expect that the phenomenon of contrast should increase during crisis, with the decision makers perceiving fewer discrepant (from their own position) communications as acceptable while increasing the number that are rejected. That is, they will more often contrast communications from an enemy or opponent rather than assimilating them. We should expect, therefore, as we found in the Russians' perception of the Chinese stand on the nuclear test ban treaty, that a group of decision makers will more likely distort the rival's position on an issue in a direction away from their own during a crisis situation. Conversely, decision makers, during periods of detenté should be expected to increase the areas of acceptance or noncommitment and reduce their latitude of rejection in evaluating communications from the opponent. In this situation the assimilating effect should be stronger with one group of decision makers distorting or, more accurately, displacing the rivals' orientations in a direction more consonant with one's own. One index, then, of a change in the direction of a crisis from escalation to deescalation would be the enlargement of the latitude of acceptance and an increase in communication assimilation with corresponding decreases in rejection and contrast.

Congruent with the work of the Sherifs is that of Scott (1966) who has pointed out that stereotypes (defined as distorted, oversimplified, or overgeneralized images) are more likely to be attached to disliked rather than to liked images. As he reports (Scott, 1966: 70)

> The holder of an image is restricted in the kinds of testing action he can take. Similarly, the object of the image is restricted in the actions he an take to change the view of the image-holder. If the ideologies of two groups are antagonistic, they produce strong forces toward the development of unrealistic images. Here, particularly, one would expect to be reinforced both by isolation from the object of the image and by the way in which information is presented through the available channels of communication. The favorable attributes of a liked object are accentuated, and so are unfavorable attributes of a disliked object.

The combined effect of a crisis or threat situation, thus, is the reduction in the cognitive richness of one's perceptions of the enemy, the emphasis within these dimensions of negative aspects (partly because of the lack of opportunity for direct contact), and a distortion of the rival's position in terms of contrasting that position with his own in a number of issue-areas, rather than assimilating them.

EXCEPTIONS TO THE BALANCE MODEL

Certain exceptions to the universality of the cognitive balance model apply most strongly to the study of international crises. Price et al. (1966) have found that when either disliking or disagreement is involved in the A-B-X bonds, the balance principle fails to hold. The only exception is the situation in which A and B hold positive orientations toward X, but their own relationship is negative. Here imbalance or uneasiness is felt.

The authors explain this gap in the model by theorizing that these imbalances could come about because of uncertainty in A's perception or cognition of the B-X relationship. They believe that when A-B is positive, an actor holds assumptions of reciprocity, but that these assumptions are not reliably made when A-B is neutral or negative, because there is apt to be much uncertainty and ambiguity. Also, when the A-B relationship is a positive one, there is also apt to be mutual concern, relevance or engagement. However, when the relationship is negative, there is a temptation to rationalize the negative feedback, minimizing the A-B or A-X bond by perceiving or labeling it as weak or of little relevance. Thus, conclude the authors, in the absence of engagement, indifference prevails over considerations of balance.

In these studies, of course, the subjects are college students who have no great motivation for disliking each other over reported disagreements in their attitudes in an experiment. In international crises one would assume that there is too much at stake for leaders to minimize the disagreements or to be afraid to face the existence of disagreements or hostile feelings. However, the principle may still be a valid one; when negative signs are part of the balance structure, there is apt to be more imbalance.

Another exception to the model is the finding by Scott (1962: 73) that dimensional simplicity produces more balanced groupings than does dimensional complexity:

> Though [structural balance] may represent a preferred state of a cognitive system, this is more likely to be true for systems of low, rather than high, dimensional complexity. The more independent dimensions a person has available for classifying a set of phenomenal objects, the less likely it is that his classifications will yield balanced groups. It is in relatively simple cognitive structures that the affective attribute is most salient, and other bases for grouping tend to be closely associated with it, thus yielding balanced groups of objects.

This observation by Scott is congruent with the Osgood and Tannenbaum (1955) finding that intense attitudes are more productive of balanced attitudinal linkages. We have cited evidence that stress reduces cognitive dimensionality and, logically at least, is conducive to intense attitudes or high ego-involvement. We should thus expect to find that stress, threat, noxity or crisis will be associated with more balanced groupings even though perceptual distortion may be necessary to produce that balance. This, of course, is a contradiction of the previous principle of imbalance being associated with mutually negative actor orientations (assuming that these are associated with threat and crisis), as Price et al. (1966) have found. The resolution of the contradiction lies in more research in a variety of situations and, in this study, the use of real or simulated international situations, rather than simulated ones using students involving purely interpersonal attitudinal issues.

Tannenbaum and Gengel (1966) have shown that imbalance may be produced by a kind of halo effect. That is, though there may be a number of A-B-X bonds in a relationship, one or several Xs of high relevance or ego-involvement may color all or many of the linkages, producing imbalances. These imbalances are minimized because they are, in fact, less relevant at the time than the dominant issue or issues which are "radiating" the halo. Tannenbaum and Gengel report that this effect accrues to both positively and negatively linked sources. The halo effect, therefore, may be found both in crisis and détente periods and thus should not affect any hypothesized differences between the two kinds of situations in terms of their proportion of balanced to imbalanced relationships.

CRISIS AND DECISION MAKERS

A question arises about the assumption that an international crisis is a situation producing stress for those involved in the making of decision affecting the onset and outcome of the crisis. Triska (1964: 8) defines a crisis as

> an extraordinary, non-routine, abnormal situation in international relations which is a result of extensive and intensive new inputs into relations among nations–inputs accelerating paces, increasing tensions, quickening responses, disbalancing stabilities, and containing elements of danger or war. It is a crucial time in which decisions, because of the high tension threshold, tend to become momentous.

But one might argue that such decision makers have built their careers around the handling of such situations and, that instead of being unnerved or thrown off balance, actually thrive on such situations. Their previous background prepares them for such situations, and they are thus emotionally attuned to their occurrence. They can deal with the exigencies of crises as a trained surgeon deals with emergency operations.

Second, crises tend to have patterns which, though decision makers may not enunciate, they more or less expect. These may not be generalized patterns which they perceive in all crises, but they are at least patterns of behavior that the decision makers have come to expect from another regime with which they have had previous dealings. In other words, they know what kinds of actions the opponent is likely to take in response to their own measures, and what measures will most likely be effective in dealing with their opponent's moves. As Triska (1964: 9) indicates

> Analytically speaking, we may assume that decision-makers cope with uncertainty of a crisis in a two-fold manner: first they assign

> priorities to alternative courses of action in terms of their own estimates of the probable outcome (or outcomes) of each alternative; and second, they act on the basis of such priorities and probabilities. If a state perceives that its priorities are "at odds" with those of another state (or other states), it may nevertheless (a) estimate that the realization of such priorities is rather probable and (b) decide to achieve such priorities by engaging in a risk situation with the other state. Probability estimates and the willingness and capability to engage in risk situations permit decision makers to cope with uncertainty.

The nonviolent resolutions of almost all the direct American-Soviet confrontations during the Cold War point to the fact that the decision-making elites of the superpowers have adjusted to their nations' roles in the postwar international system and have learned to accept, to a large degree, the role definition of the rival nation more or less as the other power sees it. Even if one of the actors should interpret these role definitions somewhat differently than his opponent, thus precipitating the crises that have occurred in this period, there are more or less prescribed ways of resolving the conflicts. Indeed, McClelland (1968) has presented evidence of the learning of a technique of "crisis management" between the leaders of the superpowers.

The resolution of conflicts may take the form of a withdrawal or a renunciation of the status right which the crisis initiator had presumed adhered to his position in the international system. Renunciation results from persuasion or threat by the rival, or the opponent's acceptance of adjustment and to the new interpretation of the role (particularly if the international system is so structured that the rivalry between the two actors is not of a zero-sum type wherein a gain for one is an equivalent loss for the other, but is instead a variable-sum game in which one strategy may bring about losses or gain for both—though not necessarily equal ones for each side). The rather passive acceptance by the Americans of the Czechoslovak invasion of 1968 is an example of the latter behavior. Soviet behavior in Eastern Europe thus becomes post hoc, albeit tacit, justification for American behavior in the Dominican Republic and, to a certain extent, even in Vietnam.

The argument, then, for maintaining that a crisis is a stressful situation bringing about cognitive rigidity and simplification leading to perceptual distortion appears to have little justification in this view. What are the arguments, then, assuming the contrary is true? One would have to maintain that for the decision makers, an international crisis is not a typical situation. In this view (Hermann, 1969) a crisis is out of the ordinary routine in terms of the specific situation (an occurrence which they did not expect), and one which makes extraordinary time and psychological demands on them. Thus analogous to the football players who train for the "big game," decision makers may also be versed in handling conflictive situations. However, the actual occurrence of a crisis creates tensions and brings about psychological changes which do not exist in non-crisis periods. As Robert Kennedy (1969: 44) states in his narrative of the events of the Cuban missile crisis

> The strain and the hours without sleep were beginning to take their toll. However, even many years later, those human weaknesses—impatience, fits of anger—are understandable. Each one of us was being asked to make a recommendation which, if wrong and if accepted, could mean the destruction of the human race. That kind of pressure does strange things to a human being, even to brilliant, self-confident, mature, experienced men. For some it brings out characteristics and strengths that perhaps even they never knew they had, and for others the pressure is overwhelming.
>
> Why does this happen?

It occurs primarily because crisis situations are brought about precisely by behavior which is somehow out-of-role, a behavioral occurrence which is not sanctioned by the norms of the international system. In other words, though the large powers may have come to recognize their respective statuses in the postwar system, adjustments are periodically necessary to maintain the system. Though decision makers may have tacitly drawn up a set of rules for dealing with these adjustments, the actual process of adjusting may sometimes be a painful one for the decision makers, mainly because the outcome is very often in doubt. As Triska (1964: 9) has indicated,

> Foreign policy decision-making has always involved an element of uncertainty for its participants. Machiavelli's advice and criticism concerning interstate relations, Bismarck's classical statement concerning the "art of the possible," and contemporary treatises on game theory all focus on this element of uncertainty.

The uncertainty of outcome combined with negative reaction to the behavior which precipitated the crisis generates hostile feelings toward the opponent. As Taylor (1968) points out, dislike of another individual creates tension (or more tension than a mutually positive one), and disagreement results in higher tension than does agreement. Thus, even though cognitive balance may be maintained (in the case of disagreement over an issue area with another to whom one is negatively oriented, or negative orientation toward one with whom one is in profound disagreement over an issue area that is important to the mutual relationship), psychological tensions are generated.

The problem is, of course, a theoretically important one, but takes on additional normative implications if the behavioral consequences of cognitive complexity coinciding with perception of threat are spelled out. Pruitt (1966: 396) does just that:

> Threat perception is often a prominent feature of the progress of events that lead to war. Actions taken by one nation to defend itself against threat are often seen as evidence of threat by the citizens of another. This may lead to defensive preparations by the other nation, which, in turn, are seen as further evidence of threat by citizens of the first. Thus international tension may develop through a circular process . . . that produces a deepening sense of threat to both sides. Such circular processes have often culminated in war, the actual outbreak taking place in a time of crisis when the sense of threat became so great on one or both sides that decision-makers lost their capacity to think clearly about the problems at hand.

Thus, hostility, disagreements and threats generated by the opponent's behavior (or more accurately, one's perception of it) bring about tensions which other aspects of the crisis only enhance. Time demands, threats of physical or prestige loss, uncertainty about the immediate outcome of the crisis, and worries over the further consequences of the outcome in other, less direct areas also heighten the tension. Thus it may be that though decision makers will not "lose their heads," the onset of a crisis does bring about a different psychological climate, which is itself sufficient to generate further escalation of the crisis, leading perhaps to all-out war in the classic pattern of World War I.

Thus the purpose of this investigation will be to apply Newcomb's A-B-X model to investigate the applicability of the model for international politics. Specifically does cognitive balance exist in national decision-making? What are the differences between crisis and noncrisis decision-making in terms of distortion (assimilation and contrast of one's own views with that of an opponent), and what effect does that have upon one's evaluation of the opponent? Does crisis lead to greater distortion of perception of the opponent's position, and, if so, what is the nature of the distortion? Is it of a type which will lead to greater escalation by maximizing differences between the two groups of decision makers, or is it one in which differences between the two groups are minimized, thus permitting or encouraging de-escalation? Are there systematic differences between the two groups; i.e., does one side distort more than the other, or does one side distort in one direction while the other does so in the opposite direction? What are the effects of crisis on the balance model itself? Does negative actor orientation lead to imbalance, either in crisis or noncrisis situations? Does crisis, because of perceptual simplification, lead to a reduction in imbalance, i.e., ambiguities which interfere with the necessity for making action? These are the questions which we want to answer by this investigation.

HYPOTHESES

The literature discussed in the above section suggests some hypotheses which are testable by a variety of content analysis techniques.

(1) The level of dimensionality of national decision maker's cognitive structures will be lower in crisis situations than in noncrisis situations.

(2) In a crisis situation, if decision makers of nation A have a positive or negative orientation toward an environmental object, X, and if they perceive that decision makers of nation B have a cognitively different orientation toward the same object, then the decision makers of nation A will have a negative orientation toward their counterparts in nation B in the context of that issue-area. Conversely, the orientation of the decision makers of nation B will be negative toward their counterparts in nation A if the former perceive that the latter's orientation toward object X differs from their own.

(3) If decision makers in a crisis period perceive that their orientations to given Xs are similar (whether positive or negative), there will be mutual positive attraction between them.

(4) During crisis, if decision makers' orientations toward each other are negative, they will distort the extent to which they perceive their opponents' orientation as differing from their own.

Definitions

(1) National decision makers are those individuals who, by virtue of their formal or informal organizational roles in the national political system can commit the resources of their nations to a course of action in the international system (see Brody, 1966; Holsti et al., 1968).

(2) Level of dimensionality refers to the relative concentration or distribution of themes "which are defined as having no more than one each of the following elements: (1) the perceiver, (2) the perceived or agent of action, (3) the action, (4) the target of the action" (North et al., 1963: 136).

DATA

The data for this study were generated from all publicly available statements, speeches, documents and letters issued by the decision makers of the United States and the Soviet Union of two time periods: the Bay of Pigs invasion in April 1961 and the Cuban missile crisis of October 1962.

All the themes from all the documents in each of the two periods were categorized according to issue-area. Twenty-seven thematic categories were thus generated (see Appendix B). Each of these categories were further divided into six perceptual subcategories, following the model discussed above. With A standing for the documents of the United States and B for the documents of the Soviet Union, these subcategories are:

A. United States Documents

(1) A–X. All themes which are United States decision makers' expressions of their attitude toward X.

(2) A-B-X. All themes which are United States decision makers' perceptions of the Soviet decision makers' relationship, action or attitude toward an X.

(3) A-B(X). All themes which are United States decision makers' expression of their orientation to the Soviet Union as an actor in the international system in the context of that issue-area.

B. Soviet Union Documents

(1) B-X. All themes which are Soviet decision makers' expression of their attitude toward an X.

(2) B-A-X. All themes which are Soviet decision makers' perceptions of the American decision makers' relationship, action or attitude toward an X.

(3) B-A(X). All themes which are Soviet decision makers' expression of their orientations to the Soviet Union as an actor in the international system in the context of that issue-area.

METHODOLOGY

The use of a scaling technique as a way of generating quantified data on perceptions of decision makers appeared as an innovative methodological step in the study of crisis. Since event scaling as a method of measuring the behavior of nations seems to have some promise, an analogous perceptual scale based on a similar rationale might also prove useful for measuring the images which groups of decision makers have of one another. Various methods of content analysis have been proposed and tested in recent years

(Holsti, 1969). The General Inquirer is one that has proved often successful (Holsti et al., 1964). However, this method is quite costly in computer time and in human labor in coding and keypunching, particularly when dealing with a large number of thematic categories and perceptual subcategories as in this study. Scaling offers flexibility and relative ease of data handling.

As Moses et al. (1967) indicate, scaling provides a way of quantitatively comparing "messages or . . . acts of a given country in two or more different" situations. The scale devised by Moses et al. and modified by Azar (1969) provides a model for the construction of a perceptual scale. The scale used in this paper follows this rationale. The construction of the scale was originally inductive; that is, the documents were scanned for the possible range of perception types one would encounter. Analogously, the perceptual continuum upon which the scale is founded is one of cooperation and conflict. Thus thirty-three perceptual message types were generated first. These ranged from those implying attitudes or perceptions of international cooperation between actors at the low end of the scale to those implying conflict and violence at the high end (see Appendix A). The perceptual types were ranked by four judges: the Spearman r between the first judge and the second, third, and fourth were .73, .65, and .83. Three types (or marker cards) which accounted for the bulk of the deviation were eliminated and three additional judges ranked the cards. The correlations between the first and the fifth, sixth and seventh rankings were .96, .97 and .97.

All the themes in each of the message types and its perceptual subcategories were scaled by the judge, and each of the themes given a score corresponding to the level of conflict which it expressed (as determined by the marker card behind which it was placed). The individual theme scores for each subcategory were averaged. Thus the overall score for each subcategory represents an average for each of the themes contained in it.

FINDINGS

Hypothesis One

The level of dimensionality can be operationalized in several ways. One of these is the degree of concentration of attention on one or a few Xs as contrasted with a dispersal of attention over a wide range of issue-areas. This presumably would increase the severity of a crisis because the decision makers' attention would be restricted to those points at conflict while they would block out those issues over which there is agreement. We decided to test the hypothesis by comparing our crisis documents with a similar set of statements and speeches made by relevant Soviet and American leaders during two noncrisis periods, the visit of Khrushchev to the United States in 1959 and the signing of the Nuclear Test Ban Treaty in 1963, and examining them for levels of attention concentration in the same issue areas. We found that there was little difference between crisis and noncrisis situations for both countries in terms of concentration with the exception of the United States in the Bay of Pigs invasion. Thus, while there may be concentration on the problem of Cuba or the blockade in the crisis periods, there is also concentration on the nuclear test ban treaty, world peace, international law and order and other aspects of détente in noncrisis situations.

Another technique for ascertaining the degree of complexity of cognitive structures is that of comparing message length with the assumption that the shorter the message, the less information is being transmitted, and that therefore greater stereotyping is occurring (Holsti, 1965: 375-376). We find support for this hypothesis using this method. The average number of themes contained in the U.S. documents for crisis periods is 56.9 as compared with 120.3 during the noncrisis periods. For the Soviets the respective figures are 78.8 and 158.0. These figures result from the aggregation of the two crisis periods and of the two noncrisis periods. If they are disaggregated, we find that for the Bay of Pigs the average message length was 87, while for the Camp David meeting it was 70.6. However, the average message length for the U.S. in the Cuban Missile crisis was 38.5, thus lowering the total average. For the Soviet Union we find a similar situation when we disaggregate. Average message length for the nuclear test ban treaty period was 87.0 as compared to 125 during the Bay of Pigs invasion. However, comparing the 61.5 average for the Cuban missile crisis to the 225.6 average for the Camp David meeting accentuates the difference sharply. Thus for the Cuban missile crisis period in particular, message length supported the hypothesis. But it is an assumption and not an empirical finding that shorter message length is an indicator of cognitive simplicity. One has to look at the content, which we do below.

Hypothesis Two

The hypothesis states that differences between one's own attitude toward an X and that perceived to be held by your opponent will lead to a negative orientation toward that opponent. This would presumably be at the core of the factors producing crisis situations. If we take those categories (9 and 11) in which the United States decision makers have positive relationship toward the X and perceive the Soviets to have a negative relationship toward the same issue-area, one (9) confirms the hypothesis while the other does not; that is, U.S. orientation to the Soviet Union is negative. in the context of 9 and positive in the context of 11. A similar situation holds true with respect to those cases (13, 17) in which the Americans have a negative relationship toward the X while perceiving the Soviet Union to have a positive relationship (with the hypothetical outcome being a negative orientation toward B). Here again, one case (13) confirms while the other (17) disconfirms. Thus, in neither category is a significant relationship established. But the case in each category corroborating the hypothesis does so dramatically–i.e., the negatively perceived dependent relationship has received a much higher score than the two independent relationships. Of course, the paucity of data for both categories makes it extremely hazardous to draw conclusions, and it seems best to suspend judgment.

For the Soviet Union, the one case in which the Soviets are positive toward the X (23) and perceive the United States to be negative toward it does confirm the hypothesis. In those cases in which the Soviets perceive the X negatively, at the same time perceiving that the United States is relating positively, two cases (6 and 25) confirm the hypothesis while three (2, 7, and 20) disconfirm it. Again, there is an even number of relationships supporting and disproving the hypothesis, though the supporting ones do so strongly. Thus, cognitive balance which in such situations leads to negative orientations during crisis seems to occur in some issue areas and not in others. With the exception of one Soviet case confirming the hypothesis, all of the other categories for both the Soviet Union and the United States, whether confirming or not, are of low salience.

Hypothesis Three

The third hypothesis states that similarities of attitudes toward given Xs will be associated with positive orientations toward the other group of decision makers. The significance of this hypothesis lies in the fact that, if confirmed, it shows that orientations, even during crisis, are issue-specific. We find that for the United States in each category (3, 4, 8, 20, 21, 22, 23 and 24) in which their orientation toward the X is positive and in which they perceive the Soviet orientation to be also positive, their orientation toward the Soviet decision makers is positive.

In those categories (1, 6, 7, 16, 17, 18) where the Americans have a negative attitude toward the X and perceive that the Soviets also have a negative image of that same X, the results are mixed. The hypothesis holds for categories 1, 6 and 17, but not for categories 7, 16 and 18. Overall, however, 11 out of the 14 cases uphold the hypothesis while three cases contradict it for the Americans.

For the Soviet Union, the situation is similar. When the Soviet Union decision makers perceive the issue-area positively and perceive that the United States perceives it in the same manner, then they will perceive the United States positively in the context of that issue-area. This is true for all five categories which fit the specifications–8, 9, 11, 14 and 15. However, when the Soviet attitude toward the X is negative and they perceive that the Americans also relate negatively toward the object (the hypothetical situation being positive Soviet orientation toward the United States in that issue-area) only one case (category 7) out of five (the other four being categories 1, 16, 17 and 20) confirms the hypothesis.

There appears, then, to be a substantial difference between orientations when attitudes are perceived to be similar and positive and when they are similar and negative. In all cases in which American and Soviet decision makers' perceptual structures are composed of positive orientations, the relations are balanced. However, when negative actor and object orientations enter the scene, the tendency toward balance is thwarted, and more cases of imbalance than balance occur. This appears to be a confirmation of the Price et al. (1966) finding that imbalances are more common among negative A–B–X relationships. Their explanation for this phenomena was that negative orientations are associated with uncertainty and ambiguity while positive relationships involve mutual concern, relevance or engagement. It is certainly true that international crisis has been associated with uncertainty and ambiguity, as we have seen, but Price et al. suggest that imbalances in negative cognitive structure are a way of rationalizing the negative feedback or minimizing the negative A–B or A–X bond. This, however, according to most crisis literature, is what should not occur. There should be an attempt to magnify the negative orientations to justify the hostility and perception of threat. Thus, the findings for both the American and Soviet decision makers in these crisis situations indicate that maintenance of their mutual relationship was more important than emphasis on the differences which divide them, even in the midst of crisis.

But we also see very clearly here that perceptual structures are issue-specific and that a depiction of the overall relationship as totally positive or negative would certainly be misleading. It is even more important to maintain the distinctions between the issue-areas in view of the differences one finds between positive and negative cognitive structures.

Hypothesis Four

The hypothesis here tests an aspect of the circular process of the escalation of negative orientations between actors. It involves the distortion of their opponents' position in a direction away from their own, which would have the effect of confirming or heightening their original negative attraction.

For U.S. perceptions we find no case where this hypothesis is confirmed. American decision makers' perceptions of Soviet orientations are either accurate or the distortion is in the direction of lessening differences. This is true whether or not the actual perceptions are discrepant in the first place.

In the one case (category 16) in which the U.S. orientation to the Soviet Union is negative and the actual attitude of the Soviet Union toward the X is negative, there is no tendency for the United States to see the orientation as more negative than it is. When the U.S. perception of the Soviet Union is negative, and the Soviet attitude toward the X is positive (category 9), the United States sees the attitude as less rather than more positive than it is.

The same is true for the Soviet Union. In those cases (1 and 23) in which the Soviets perceive the American orientation negatively while the U.S. leaders perceive the issue-area as positive, the Soviets see the American position as less positive than it actually is. Again, for those categories (6, 11, 17) in which the Soviet orientation toward the United States is negative, and the U.S. is negative, the Soviets perceive the U.S. position to be less negative than it actually is.

Here again we find evidence that the crisis perception of both parties follows a pattern more akin to a détente period than to crisis. The results indicate that both parties had widened their area of acceptance and narrowed the area of rejection, evidence that the positions on both sides were not extreme ones. The lack of extreme commitment would permit both parties to perceive the other's positions accurately or actually to assimilate them. This would encourage both parties to minimize existing differences and to submerge them in an attempt to hook onto mutual areas of positive orientations, permitting a resolution of the conflict.

CONCLUSIONS

The results show mixed support for the hypotheses. The hypothesis concerning level of dimensionality was both supported and not supported depending on the indicator used. The second hypothesis (relating differences in attitudes to negative orientations) had mixed results, although this is the area in which one would expect to gather the bulk of findings for crisis studies. Surprisingly, we find instead stronger confirmation for our second hypothesis in relating similarities in attitudes to positive actor orientations. Furthermore, the hypothesis is most strongly confirmed by cases in which not only similarities in attitudes but similarities of positive attitudes were associated with positive orientations. Again, the third hypothesis fails to show distortion of one's opponents' attitudes in a direction away from one's own, except in the case of the Soviet distortion of the negativeness of the American attitude toward the Castro regime. In all the other cases, if distortion does take place, it is in the direction of distorting toward one's own viewpoint, a trend which one would not expect in an international crisis situation.

The bulk of the evidence is in the direction of regarding both Cuban crises as examples of a process of crisis adaptation. Instead of uncovering evidence of mutual distortion of one's rivals' positions, of balanced negative perceptual configurations (justifying hostile behavior), and of wide latitudes of rejection leading to exaggeration of mutual attitudinal discrepancies, the opposite was found. The discovery of imbalance in negative cognitive structures while finding balance predominating in positive cognitive structures leads us to believe that a perceptual search for certainty and unambiguity was undertaken by both parties to the crises. This search did not, however, lead to a self-encapsulating reinforcement of each group's more hostile and distorted perceptions (see Janis, 1971), but to a move away from extreme commitments, thus allowing perceptions of the other side's positions to be assimilated toward one's own (thus creating distortion, but in the direction opposite to that expected under crisis circumstances). These findings would indicate that an avoidance of extreme commitments led to perceptual consequences emphasizing mutual concern and reciprocity rather than to hostility and conflict escalation.

Other studies of the Cuban missile crisis (see Holsti et al., 1969) indicate that the Soviet and American decision makers perceived each other's behavior accurately and were mutually responsive to deescalatory moves. The studies of the Cuban missile crisis by the Stanford group emphasize the process of crisis management which McClelland (1968: 165) also discusses, as mentioned above. Thus, one is left with two choices in approaching the study of crisis: one, that the Bay of Pigs and Cuban missile crisis are anomalies in that they did not result in large scale violence as did the crises preceding the outbreak of World War I, the Korean War or the bombing of North Vietnam; or two, that the Cuban crises (the latter, in particular) were just one of a series of episodes occurring since the end of World War II in which the United States and the Soviet Union have confronted each other over an issue. In the process of confrontation (in which new relationships within and between polar blocs are redefined) a learning process has occurred in which each side has developed various expectations concerning its rival's probable behavior if a threshold of violence is crossed. Thus as McClelland (1968) indicates, the range of behaviors which is found in U.S.-Soviet confrontations over time has contracted and become more responsive. He labels this process "routinization" of crisis, implying that, though hostile interactions increase during specific periods, they are always kept in bounds which the decision makers of both sides have tacitly drawn.

Routinization on the perceptual level means that the decision makers have come to perceive their rivals within a framework which though permitting occurrences of threat, surprise, and short decision time (see Hermann, 1969), is nevertheless oriented to a limitation of the confrontation within certain levels of conflict. Perceptual distortion which minimizes rather than increases issue differences aids in this conflict limitation. Cognitive imbalances within negative perceptual structures also indicate a tendency toward certainty and reciprocity, major characteristics of crisis routinization and adaptation.

Methodologically the study has shown that a technique analogous to Azar's (1970) and McClelland's (and Hoggard, 1969) event data categorizations can be developed and fruitfully employed in the study of decision makers's perceptions. Care must be taken to achieve a high level of agreement, not only in the scaling of individual themes, but most importantly in the coding of the perceptual subcategories. The difference in operational respects between an A–B–X or B–A–X bond on one hand, and an A–B(X) or B–A(X), can be quite subtle and not easy to discern readily. Since the advantage of this method over the Stanford General Inquirer is in its economy and is proposed as a complementary method, it would prove useful to compare the results applying both techniques to the same data sources. This will be done in a later study.

NOTE

1. As an illustration of this principle, I found in previous work (Adelman, 1964) that a high positive orientation toward an X (in this case, Soviet decision makers' highly positive attitude toward the nuclear test ban treaty) was associated with distortion of the differences between their own position and that of the rival actor (in this case China's moderately negative attitude toward the treaty). In other words, the Soviet leaders, because they were positively oriented toward the treaty, were propelled to magnify the extent of the Chinese deviation from their own orientation. The Chinese, on the other hand, were only predominantly negative (in contrast to the Soviets' overwhelmingly positive orientation) so that there was not the psychological inducement of strain on the part of the Chinese to contrast so greatly their own orientation to that of the Soviets.

REFERENCES

ADELMAN, M. (1964) "Perceived nonconsensus in an international subsystem." Stanford University Department of Political Science. (mimeo)

ALKER, H. A., Jr. (1964) "Dimensions of conflict in the General Assembly." Am. Pol. Sci. Rev. 58 (September): 642-657.

AZAR, E. E. (1970) "Analysis of international events." Peace Research Reviews 21 (November): 1-113.

--- (1969) "Gathering and measuring phenotypic events in the study of international political unification." Michigan State University. (mimeo)

BRODY, R. A. (1966) "Cognition and behavior: a model of international relations," in O. J. Harvey (ed.) Experience, Structure, and Adaptation. New York: Springer.

BRUNER, J. S. (1958) "Social psychology and perception," pp. 85-94 in E. E. Maccoby et al. (eds.) Readings in Social Psychology. New York: Holt, Rinehart & Winston.

DAHL, R. A. (1961) Who Governs? Democracy and Power in an American City. New Haven: Yale Univ. Press.

DRIVER, M. J. (1965) "A cognitive structure analysis of aggression, stress, and personality in an inter-national simulation." Purdue University. (mimeo)

FESTINGER, L., S. SCHACTER, and M. BACK (1950) Social Pressures in Informal Groups. New York: Harper.

HEIDER, F. (1946) "Attitudes and cognitive organization." J. of Psychology 21: 107-112.

HERMANN, C. F. (1969) Crises in Foreign Policy: A Simulation Analysis. Indianapolis: Bobbs-Merrill.

HOLSTI, O. R. (1969) Content Analysis for the Social Sciences and Humanities. Reading, Mass.: Addison-Wesley.

--- (1967) "Cognitive dynamics and images of the enemy." J. of International Affairs 21: 16-39.

--- (1965) "The 1914 case." Am. Pol. Sci. Rev. 59 (June): 365-378.

---, R. A. BRODY, and R. C. NORTH (1969) "Measuring affect and action in international reaction models: empirical materials from the 1962 Cuban crisis," pp. 679-696 in J. N. Rosenau (ed.) International Politics and Foreign Policy. New York: Free Press.

--- (1964) "Theory and measurement of inter-state relations." Stanford University Studies in International Conflict and Integration. (unpublished)

HOLSTI, O. R., R. C. NORTH, and R. A. BRODY (1968) "Perception and action in the 1914 crisis," pp. 123-158 in J. D. Singer (ed.) Quantitative International Politics: Insights and Evidence. New York: Free Press.

JANIS, I. L. (1971) "Groupthink." Psychology Today 5 (November): 43-46.

KENNEDY, R. F. (1969) Thirteen Days: A Memoir of the Cuban Missile Crisis. New York: NAL.

McCLELLAND, C. A. (1968) "Access to Berlin: the quantity and variety of events, 1948-1963," pp. 159-186 in J. D. Singer (ed.) Quantitative International Politics. New York: Free Press.

--- and G. HOGGARD (1969) "Conflict patterns among nations," pp. 711-724 in J. N. Rosenau (ed.) International Politics and Foreign Policy. New York: Free Press.

MOSES, L. E., R. A. BRODY, O. R. HOLSTI, J. B. KADANE, and J. S. MILSTEIN (1967) "Scaling data on inter-nation action." Science 56 (May 26): 1054-1059.

NEWCOMB, T. M. (1959) "The study of consensus," pp. 277-299 in R. K. Merton et al. (eds.) Sociology Today: Problems and Prospects. New York: Basic Books.

--- (1958) "Communicative behavior," pp. 244-265 in R. Young (ed.) Approaches to the Study of Politics. Evanston, Ill.: Northwestern Univ. Press.

--- (1953) "An approach to the study of communicative acts." Psych. Rev. 60: 393-404.

NORTH, R. C. (1968) "The behavior of nation-states: problems of conflict and integration," pp. 303-356 in M. Kaplan (ed.) New Approaches to International Relations. New York: St. Martin's Press.

--- O. R. HOLSTI, M. G. ZANINOVICH, and D. A. ZINNES (1963) Content Analysis. Evanston, Ill.: Northwestern Univ. Press.

OSGOOD, C. E. and P. TANNENBAUM (1955) "The principle of congruity in the prediction of attitude change." Psych. Rev. 60: 42-46.

PRICE, L. E., E. HARBURG, and T. M. NEWCOMB (1966) "Psychological balance in situations of negative interpersonal attitudes." J. of Personality and Social Psychology 3: 265-270.

PRUITT, D. G. (1966) "Definition of the situation as a determinant of international action," pp. 391-432 in H. C. Kelman (ed.) International Behavior: A Social-Psychological Analysis. New York: Holt, Rinehart & Winston.

ROBINSON, J. A. and R. C. SNYDER (1966) "Decision-making in international politics," pp. 433-463 in H. C. Kelman (ed.) International Behavior: A Social-Psychological Approach. New York: Holt, Rinehart & Winston.

ROSENBERG, M. J., C. I. HOVLAND, W. J. McGUIRE, R. P. ABELSON, and J. W. BREHM (1960) Attitude Organization and Change. New Haven: Yale Univ. Press.

RUSSETT, B. M. (1966) "Discovering voting groups in the United Nations." Am. Pol. Sci. Rev. 60 (June): 327-339.

SCHROEDER, H. J., M. J. DRIVER, and S. STREUFERT (1967) Human Information Processing: Individuals and Groups Functioning in Complex Social Situations. New York: Holt, Rinehart & Winston.

SCOTT, W. A. (1966) "Psychological and social correlates of international images," pp. 70-103 in H. C. Kelman (ed.) International Behavior: A Social-Psychological Analysis. New York: Holt, Rinehart & Winston.

--- (1962) "Cognitive complexity and cognitive balance." Sociometry 26: 66-74.

SHERIF, C., M. SHERIF, and R. NEGERBALL (1965) Attitude and Attitude Change: The Social Judgment-Involvement Approach. Philadelphia: W. B. Saunders.

SHERIF, M. (1967) "Attitude as the individual's own categories: the social judgment-involvement approach to attitude change," pp. 105-140 in M. Sherif and C. Sherif (eds.) Attitude, Ego-Involvement, and Change. New York: John Wiley.

--- and C. I. HOVLAND (1961) Social Judgment: Assimilation and Contrast Effects in Communication and Attitude Change. New Haven: Yale Univ. Press.

SHERIF, M. with C. SHERIF (1967) "The social judgment-involvement approach to attitude and attitude change," in M. Sherif (ed.) Social Interaction: Process and Products. Chicago: Aldine.

SNYDER, R. C., H. W. BRUCK and B. SAPIN [eds.] (1966) Foreign Policy Decision Making: An Approach to the Study of International Politics. New York: Free Press.

TANNENBAUM, P. H. and R. W. GENGEL (1966) "Generalization of attitude change through congruity principle relationships." J. of Personality and Social Psychology 3: 299-304.

TAYLOR, H. F. (1968) "Balance tension and tension release in the two person group." Human Relations 21 (February): 59-74.

TRISKA, J. F. (1964) "Pattern and level of risk in Soviet foreign policy making." Stanford University Studies of the Communist System 4.

APPENDIX A
THE PERCEPTION SCALE

1. Nation A declares the necessity of having peace and security throughout the world.
2. Nation A scores a propaganda victory through the accomplishment of an action.
3. Nation A extends technical aid to Nation B.
4. Nations A, B . . . hold a conference about some important matters vital to world security and peace.
5. Nation A calls for a "cease-fire" in some action.
6. Nation A offers to negotiate with Nation B over a particular issue on which they differ.
7. An official representative of Nation A offers "all and any possible assistance" in bringing some outstanding problems and differences with Nations B, C . . . to quick and mutually satisfying conclusions.
8. In response to a threat from Nation A, Nation B halts some specific activity in which it has been engaging.
9. Nations A, B . . . engage in the joint construction of weapons maintenance and storage facilities.
10. Nation A withdraws from some international organization.
11. Nation A calls an emergency meeting of its cabinet or other such security organization.
12. Nation A exchanges notes of "important diplomatic content" with Nation B over some matter.
13. Nation A declares a promise of "support and assistance" to nation X with its problems with Nation B.
14. Nations A, X . . . enemies of Nation B join in mutual denunciation of some action of Nation B and promise "complete support and assistance" to prevent the reoccurrence of such action.
15. Nation A makes diplomatic threats against Nation B over some matter.
16. Nation A increases its military aid to Nation X.
17. Nation A accuses of Nation B of planning some action (such as preemptive war) against them.
18. Nation A denies Nation B's allegations of some act(s).
19. Nation A sends a note of protest to Nation B concerning some alleged act of Nation B.
20. Nation A rejects Nation B's note of protest.
21. Nation A demands that Nation B halt some activity.
22. Nation A imposes further internal controls upon its own society.
23. Nation A demands that Nation B "cease and desist" from some action, threatening Nation B "in some manner" if it does not do so.
24. Nation A senses a "loss of security" from some act of Nation B.
25. Nation A justifies some action in the name of "national security."
26. Nation A initiates a "quarantine" of some kind against Nation B.
27. Nation A establishes a blockade against Nation B.
28. Units of Nation A confront armed units of Nation B over some important matter.
29. Nation A engages in "limited war action" with Nation B.
30. Nation A (or its alleged representatives) engage in open conflict against Nation B.

APPENDIX B
CODE FOR DOCUMENT CONTENT ANALYSIS

A = U.S. regime
B = USSR regime
X1 = Cuban regime = Castro
X2 = Cuban regime = Batista
X3 = Cuban people
X4 = Cuban rebels
X5 = Missiles in Turkey
X6 = World peace and international law, peaceful great power relations
X7 = Danger of war, arms races
X8 = Political and economic progress including Alliance for Progress, peaceful uses of atomic energy
X9 = Western Hemisphere-Latin America
X10 = De Gaulle
X11 = United Nations
X12 = NATO and U.S. allies other than OAS
X13 = OAS
X14 = USSR people
X15 = U.S. people
X16 = Weapons in Cuba
X17 = U.S. blockage and related actions
X18 = International communism
X19 = Third World
X20 = Humanity
X21 = Nuclear test ban and disarmament, summit meetings
X22 = Historical personality of USSR
X23 = Historical personality of U.S.
X24 = Laos-Southeast Asia
X25 = China
X26 = Berlin and German reunification
X0 = Other

APPENDIX C
SCALING RESULTS

Thematic Category	Perceptual Subcategories				
	A-X	A-B-X	A-B(X)	n	%
Nation A					
1	11	27	5	461	.264
2	12	—	—	.13	.007
3	3	4	5	86	.049
4	8	5	6	139	.080
5	—	—	—	0	.000
6	14	20	5	56	.032
7	13	18	11	92	.053
8	3	1	1	14	.008
9	9	16	19	54	.031
10	5	—	7	4	.002
11	9	14	8	61	.035

APPENDIX C (Continued)

12	13	7	8	16	.009
13	18	7	20	33	.019
14	–	3	3	2	.001
15	8	–	–	19	.011
16	27	18	23	224	.128
17	29	13	7	59	.033
18	19	14	14	117	.067
19	–	–	–	0	.000
20	5	4	2	64	.037
21	5	5	5	31	.018
22	4	5	4	54	.031
23	7	6	7	46	.025
24	6	6	8	53	.030
25	–	–	–	0	.000
26	–	–	–	0	.000
27	–	–	–	37	.021

Nation B	B-X	B-A-X	B-A(X)	n	%
1	12	21	14	159	.156
2	14	9	9	5	.045
3	19	18	–	51	.050
4	26	19	–	50	.050
5	11	10	1	16	.016
6	14	6	16	107	.105
7	18	13	7	151	.148
8	3	2	2	10	.010
9	10	3	3	14	.014
10	–	–	–	0	.000
11	10	1	9	55	.054
12	13	12	–	7	.007
13	–	–	–	0	.000
14	1	1	1	46	.045
15	8	5	5	8	.008
16	25	15	15	41	.040
17	29	18	23	62	.061
18	–	17	9	3	.003
19	–	–	–	0	.000
20	17	12	11	61	.060
21	5	–	–	95	.093
22	12	9	5	27	.027
23	7	12	25	30	.029
24	–	–	–	0	.000
25	17	6	14	10	.010
26	15	–	–	9	.008

JOHN H. SIGLER was born in Indianapolis in 1932. He received his undergraduate education at Dartmouth College, his M.A. degree from Georgetown University, and his Ph.D. in international politics from the University of Southern California. He spent the 1953-1954 year as a Fulbright Scholar at the University of Grenoble. He is the author of articles in International Studies Quarterly *and other professional periodicals. Previously a faculty member at the University of Southern California and at Macalester College, he is now at Carleton University in Ottawa.*

JOHN OSGOOD FIELD was born in New York City in 1940. He received his undergraduate education at Harvard College, and his graduate degrees in political science from Stanford University. Currently a research associate at the Center for International Studies, Massachusetts Institute of Technology, he is the author of articles on American politics which have appeared in the American Political Science Review *and* Public Opinion Quarterly. *Two books and several articles are in progress on politicization and election dynamics in India. NAZLI CHOUCRI, an assistant professor of political science at Massachusetts Institute of Technology, received her Ph.D. from Stanford University, and has written articles on international alignments and non-alignment, and forecasting methodologies. WILLIAM C. MITCHELL received his professional training at Stanford University and the University of Chicago, from which he is currently on leave; he is a computer specialist with Fields, Grant and Company, a social science research firm in California.*

MURRAY L. ADELMAN was born in Philadelphia in 1936. He received his undergraduate education at Reed College, his M.A. degree in Russian area studies from Harvard University, and is completing work on his Ph.D. in political science at Stanford University. He has taught at Michigan State University, and is now teaching in Germany for the European Programs of the School of Politics and International Relations, University of Southern California.